Special Praise for *Disentangle*

"Sadly, this book is greatly needed. Too many of us have been raised in a manner that, due to not developing a strong sense of self, we lose ourselves seeking our value and worth, and even our identity, in relationship with others. Nancy Johnston does a beautiful job of helping the reader to both understand and be compassionate toward our self-defeating behaviors that reinforce this while offering a path toward building and claiming our *self*. Personally, I found myself underlining much of what was written as a way of holding onto the thoughts long after the read. For me that is the sign of an important book."

Claudia Black, PhD, author of *Unspoken Legacy: Addressing the Impact of Trauma and Addiction within the Family*

"Our very souls desire freedom. When caught in a trap, an addiction, or a tangle, we long for a way out, a way back to freedom. Nancy Johnston brings the voice of her recovering self to her book, *Disentangle: When You've Lost Your Self in Someone Else.* She advocates a four-pronged approach (Facing Illusions, Detaching, Setting Healthy Boundaries, and Developing Spirituality) to the process of finding our lost selves. Her book is rooted in evidence-based practice and practical skills, and she perfectly balances them with spirituality, self- disclosure, and client stories. It is clear that the author has lived this experience and that she offers her years of life, recovery, and clinical practice in a very healthful way. This book has been a real asset to my recovery and the recovery of my clients."

Margaret L. Cress, LMFT

"Nancy writes in a way that speaks to me, in a way that I can clearly understand and relate to. Not only have I read and re-read *Disentangle*, I have shared it with many friends and family members. I appreciate the sense that Nancy has lived this, continues to learn, and continues to share!"

Jerri Shannon, CSAC, Caron Treatment Centers

"As a person who has long sought a therapeutic model for addressing codependency over the past thirty-odd years, I find the approaches Nancy Johnston lays out in this second edition of her book to be refreshing. Her explanation of separating 'my problems/goals from other's problems/goals' is enlightening. Giving up one's 'self' to save a relationship deserves our close attention. I can relate since I believe that 'addiction to love' can be devastating to all of us."

Ron Pritchard, CSAC, CAS, NCACII

"Nancy Johnston has created a format that explains clearly why the basic goal for every human being is to find the self in body, mind, and spirit. She covers life experiences that form human beings from childhood onward, especially relationships that teach us to react rather than act, to fear rather than focus on the moment, to have illusions and entanglements. It is a comprehensive book, geared to help the reader unlock the reality of situations and to discover why and how we become entangled with others rather than knowing ourselves."

Judy Light Ayyildiz, author of eleven books in five genres including *Nothing but Time: A Triumph over Trauma*

DISENTANGLE

DISENTANGLE

*When You've
Lost Your Self in
Someone Else*

NANCY L. JOHNSTON

CENTRAL RECOVERY PRESS

LAS VEGAS

Central Recovery Press (CRP) is committed to publishing exceptional materials addressing addiction treatment, recovery, and behavioral healthcare topics.

For more information, visit www.centralrecoverypress.com.

First edition 2011.
Second edition 2020.

Publisher: Central Recovery Press
            3321 N. Buffalo Drive
            Las Vegas, NV 89129

25 24 23 22 21 20   1 2 3 4 5

Library of Congress Cataloging-in-Publication Data

Names: Johnston, Nancy L., author.
Title: Disentangle : when you've lost your self in someone else / Nancy L.
   Johnston, MS, LPC, LSATP, MAC.
Description: Second edition. | Las Vegas : Central Recovery Press, [2019] |
   Includes bibliographical references.
Identifiers: LCCN 2019019480 (print) | LCCN 2019022356 (ebook) | ISBN
   9781949481341 (pbk. : alk. paper)
Subjects: LCSH: Codependency literature. | Interpersonal relations--Moral
   and ethical aspects. | Autonomy (Psychology)--Moral and ethical aspects.
   | Conduct of life.
Classification: LCC RC569.5.C63 J64 2019 (print) | LCC RC569.5.C63
   (ebook) | DDC 616.86--dc23
LC record available at https://lccn.loc.gov/2019019480
LC ebook record available at https://lccn.loc.gov/2019022356

Photo of Nancy L. Johnston by Grace DuVal. Used with permission.

Publisher's Note: *Disentangle* is designed to provide accurate and valuable information about the subject matter presented. The material and approach come from the author's personal history, as well as her work as a psychotherapist over more than three decades. However, it is in no way intended to serve as a substitute for professional behavioral health services. In the event that such services are needed, a licensed professional should be consulted.

Cover design by The Book Designers and interior by Sara Streifel.

TABLE OF CONTENTS

WHEN YOU'VE LOST YOUR SELF IN SOMEONE ELSE

TANGLES

UNTANGLING

WHEN YOU'VE FOUND YOUR SELF

PREFACE

This is the third Preface I have written for *Disentangle* — not because I can't seem to get it right, but because this is the third phase of the life of this book that has taken root and keeps growing.

The seeds of *Disentangle* began in the mid-1990's as a product of both personal and professional work. I was engaged in my own recovery program for loss of self in others, participating in therapy and a twelve-step fellowship. As I began to understand the dynamics of loss of self through my inside work, I noticed my clients were asking me questions about their growth that I could best answer with the skills I was learning. I started to see how we become entangled with others and lose our self in the process. Our mental health can be dramatically affected by this loss. A list of ideas for disentangling emerged as I saw this theme in my personal and clinical work. By 2003, that list became a self-published book. I offered workshops and presentations on the book. I made a few attempts to find a traditional publisher, but my full-time work as a mental health therapist was my priority. I did not have the time to work on submissions, and frankly, I just wanted to keep teaching and developing the material.

The second phase of *Disentangle*'s life evolved in the fall of 2009. I was in my office seeing clients and returning phone calls—a regular day. One of the calls was a client asking for information about the use of medications to treat addiction. I said I had just seen an article in a professional magazine on this topic and would find it and get back with them. I immediately did. In the process of looking through the magazine, I found an announcement about Central Recovery Treatment and specifically about Central Recovery Press. That press was news to me, great news! With some researching of Central Recovery Press and ultimately a submission to them, *Disentangle* was accepted for publication and released in 2011.

Over the years since then, I have continued to teach and develop the material in this book—presenting at conferences, teaching at workshops and weekend retreats, and using the insights and ideas in my clinical work. I practice what I write about on a daily basis and have learned more about my self and the challenges of acting on what I learn. I believe in this process of finding, cultivating, and caring for self. I believe it is possible and imperative for our health and our relationships to have a healthy self from which we operate. I also have continued to read and study new material in our fields of mental health and addiction, and those learnings find their way into the content of *Disentangle*.

In the spring of 2018, Central Recovery Press asked me to write a 2nd edition of *Disentangle*. I was so pleased! They knew I had new material for the book and had expanded the ways I understand and teach its content. And we all continue to believe strongly in the value of what it has to offer for self-recovery. The third phase of *Disentangle*'s life was taking form and has grown over these past two years as I have written it, offering at least fifty percent new material to you, the reader.

You may be wondering if this book is about codependence. It is, and more profoundly, it is about the fundamental issue of loss of self that is a core feature of codependence. The clinical dynamics of codependence are real, yet the word and its definition remain controversial and little research has yet been done on it. I suggest we not get stopped by the word "codependence." I suggest that looking at loss of self in someone else is a useful way to understand what may be causing our anxiety, depression, addictions, and/ or relationship problems, and it points the way to clear, effective ways to recover our self and find balance within and without.

As you may notice, I am separating the word "self" from pronouns such as "my" and "your." This is intentional. I want to emphasize the word "self." It is what this book is about, and I am interested in helping the reader keep that word, that concept, that important reality in mind. *Disentangle* is about finding our "self" when we have lost it in someone else. It is about learning how to connect with our "self" and then knowing how to respond to it in ways that make us stronger, clearer, and more serene.

Throughout the book you will hear the voices of people who have been on this healing path and have shared their progress with me over many years. I've known them through counseling, workshops, weekend retreats, and twelve-step fellowships. They are of varied ages and walks of life. They are not named. They need not be named. They speak for many of us.

Interspersed throughout *Disentangle* you will find experiential exercises that provide valuable opportunities to practice applying the material to your life. I encourage you to complete these exercises in a separate journal. They will help you expand your awareness and build skills toward healthier relationships with others, and with your self.

Many people have been involved in my life and in the writing of this book, both directly and indirectly, and I cannot adequately acknowledge them all. So with deep gratitude, I say "Thank you!" to the dear souls who have spent time with me listening, reflecting, teaching, sharing, discussing, laughing, editing, and encouraging. You know who you are.

As for a book dedication, *Disentangle* is gratefully offered by me to each of you who want to make your life better by taking the time, energy, and courage to look at your self and by making changes that can center, clarify, and strengthen you as you live with and love people in your life. This book is not about changing them. It's about changing you so that you can enjoy your relationships, your life, and especially your self.

May *Disentangle* and each of us keep growing.

Nancy L. Johnston
March, 2020

"Every damn time I get in a relationship, I am no longer me."

WHEN YOU'VE LOST YOUR SELF IN SOMEONE ELSE

"I'm losing who I was before I met her."

"I'm not me when I'm around them."

"I do not like who I am with him."

"As years went on I slowly lost my identity.
I gave up things I loved to do."

"I don't understand why I so readily
gave up my self for them."

TANGLES

as described by various people along the way

"I attach my self to the other person . . .
that relationship is first and foremost."

"The last eight years are a haze—
like I didn't exist in my own right."

"When he left me, I was distraught in a major
way and was helpless to know what to do."

"It just wore me down."

"He melts me. He has this sick hold on me."

"I don't know who the hell I am anymore."

"I felt like I gave my self away."

"I can't seem to get back to me."

1 BY DEFINITION

Disentangle: To find your self when you are lost in someone else. To create emotional balance and centeredness within you so you can see the realities of your situation and make healthy decisions about it. To not necessarily leave/ divorce/end a relationship, but rather to cultivate a healthy self so you can then decide what to do for you and about the relationship in which you are entangled.

When we are emotionally overinvolved with another person, we lose our self and our way. Our thoughts focus on the other person, whether we want them to or not. We may justify these thoughts, believing that if we don't worry about the other person, fix things for them, plan their lives, or do what they ask, things will be just terrible. Sometimes these thoughts become paralyzing. We can think of nothing else; we feel we must do something immediately to be in contact with the other person and impact their lives (and our lives of course, though we do not necessarily see this at first). We feel awful—nervous, anxious, and agitated. We set aside important work. We set aside important people. We set aside our self.

As the entanglements progress, we lose our way. Our interactions with the other person become more complicated, angrier, more frustrating, and confusing. We believe that more of this behavior, more trying to explain and resolve a given problem, will produce the results we desire. So, we continue on and on. And things just get worse. Everyone is upset; no one is getting what they think they want. We are entangled.

Entanglements can happen in various relationships. We may be entangled with our partner, our parents, our children, our bosses. We can become entangled with clerks in stores, with the call-center person handling our complaints, with the driver of the car beside us. An entanglement can occur with anyone when we lose our centeredness in our interactions with them. We don't have to be related to the person, we don't even have to know their name, to suddenly become emotionally attached to making our point, to defending our self, or to getting them to do something we think they should do. And often we can't seem to let go of these thoughts and feelings. Our focus narrows, and our blood pressure rises.

This book is about how to stop the self-destructive process of entanglement, how to retrieve our self when we are sliding into an interpersonal tangle or, worse yet, are already caught in its web. It describes a process for people who want to break free emotionally from relationships that are unhealthy for them. This process has its roots in what we have learned about people living with addiction, and throughout the book I refer to this kinship with addiction. The issues present in relationships where addiction plays a role are often the same those living in other unhealthy relationships deal with. This includes people who:

- Are dealing with codependency.

- Are living with the addiction of someone else.

- Are living with the chronic illness of someone else.

- Are caregivers to children and/or to aging family members.

- Are being emotionally or physically hurt in their relationships.

- Are driven to fix others.

- Want to get out of a relationship and don't believe they can.

- Feel they have to be in full control of everything.

- Take care of others more than themselves.

- Mold themselves according to how they think others want them to be.

- Are unable to say no.

- Focus more on the external than the internal.

This book is about how to apply the process of disentangling in our lives. While we describe entanglement as being lost in another person, we know we can become lost in any number of things, including work, parenting, technology, food, and spending. This book will help you understand loss of self in interpersonal relationships, and will teach you skills for disentangling which can be readily applied to other things in your life.

This book is itself a product of my own work to disentangle. It has developed as I have. I write from my personal history as well as my work as a mental health and addiction counselor. My personal journey brought me to these issues initially, and the substance of this book would be sorely impoverished, and somewhat dishonest, if I did not share that history first.

"I would give anything to be the person he wants to be with."

2 SIXTY-SIX YEARS

I am now sixty-six years old. I have been consciously working on and with my self for several decades. When I am "in good form," I experience the benefits of connection to my self, and operate in a responsive rather than a reactive way. Both my relationships and I benefit from a more centered, thought-full me. Serenity can be mine.

I have learned the skills discussed here over time, from the inside out, and it hasn't always been easy. I believe, however, that sharing bits and pieces from my sixty-six years will enable me to explain this loss and finding of self with greater ease and deeper understanding.

The First Twenty-or-So Years

When I was in the seventh grade, I liked two boys, both of them the troublemakers of the class. They were cute and funny. They would call me up at night, and we'd be on the phone for hours, not saying much. I was so glad when they called. Though charmed by their rebelliousness and carefree behavior, I never got in trouble with them. They never asked me to. I just vicariously enjoyed their "wildness," while I myself was a straight-A student and held class offices.

By ninth grade I'd started seeing the guy I would eventually marry. We dated all through high school and college. On a few occasions, we broke up. When this happened, I would go out with the notorious school troublemaker, who showed little to no respect for me but whose attention I deeply desired.

But my steady boyfriend was devoted to me. He worked hard and gave me nice things. For many years, it was "safe" for me to be with him. My family loved him, as did my high-school and college friends. He was a sociable guy with a good sense of humor. Dating him, I didn't have to deal with the decisions, rejections, and disappointments of dating other people. I didn't have to think about me, my values, my identity, or my beliefs; I was able to mindlessly be in a respectable and pleasing relationship. I thought I was happy.

We were married two years. As a husband he remained the fun-loving, generally attentive guy I had dated, and he offered comfort and companionship. I believe, however, that I was just not comfortable with the idea of being married. I was in grad school in those years and working in a psychiatric hospital. We lived in a townhouse in an urban area and had fun making it home. But I did not feel quite right with things.

My doubts about being married grew. Over time I came to see essential differences in the way my husband and I liked to spend time, in the company we kept, and in some of our values. We decided to end the marriage.

I had no idea then that I was working on finding my self. Looking back, I see that a voice in me, though it hardly knew the words, wanted me to know I could not simply keep following external expectations, whether real or imagined. I was living my life mindlessly, though if you'd asked me then I would have said I was focused and purposeful. I'd always been a successful student, worker, and daughter, someone who tried very hard to please many people and seemed to succeed at it. I was rarely "in trouble." My life looked pretty good, and in many ways felt pretty good, as I reaped the benefits of my successes.

But inside, things were confused and unsettled. I needed to do something different.

I finished my master's degree, and a new job took me to the Shenandoah Valley, about three hours from my childhood home. I knew I wanted to get out of the city and into the country; what I didn't know was that I also wanted to get some physical space for my self.

It wasn't until then that I realized how much I'd been influenced by my desire to please others. I cared so much about keeping my parents, my teachers, and my friends happy with me. I feared their disapproval and their anger. I hated having anyone mad at me; it meant feeling bad and wrong. I almost always tried to be good and to do things "right."

"Right" meant doing things according to the books, according to spoken and unspoken "shoulds." "Right" meant "Do as I say." It certainly also meant being moral and ethical, of course, and I am comfortable with that. It's just that my actions, my decisions and behaviors, were governed by watching that person I was trying to please, then selecting a response or course of action that seemed to be what *they* wanted. And I mean I literally watched. I watched their faces and their behaviors for clues about how *I thought* they were feeling toward me. I wanted to know what they wanted from me, what would please them, what would make them happy, what would keep them from being angry with me.

To begin my escape from this pattern, moved by the small, internal voice that said this would be something *I* would like to do, I came to live in the Valley. And I was blessed by my ability to do so.

One of the good things about that move was that it put me in a community in which I have been very happy for many decades.

Another was that I met the man who would become my second husband, to whom I am still married. It was my relationship with this man that at first led me to yet greater depths of "lostness in the other," then subsequently to finding my way out.

The Second Twenty-or-So Years

During my first years here in the Shenandoah Valley, I frolicked in my insanity unknowingly. By day I worked as the counselor-of-delinquents; by night I took dance classes and acted in summer stock theater. I fixed up my home, socialized with new friends, and enjoyed my cats.

In many ways the times were good, just what I needed for autonomy and identity development. Granted, we know these tasks belong to the adolescent phase of development, but I didn't really get around to them until my twenties. Prior to this I had appeared independent, but there was little independent thought and substance to me. I was driven by my need to please others, to avoid conflict, and, as my work supervisor described it, to be "obsessively over-responsible."

I dated some men, and threw away one or two potentially good, loving relationships with seemingly stable men who cared about me. One in particular asked me to marry him, envisioning a lovely, festive wedding in our quaint community—this was more than I could bear. So, I left him for another. How he must have wondered what the hell was wrong with me! It has taken me a long time to figure that one out.

The man I left him for was the man who became my second husband. I was attracted to him the first time I met him. He'd stopped by my office inquiring where to go for the evening shift; he was a new temp in the building. I gave him the information he requested, and he went on his way. I wondered who he was and where he'd come from. I felt almost instantly off-balance.

Before long, I started to get to know him through mutual friends, learning bits and pieces here and there. He had come to this area to live with a friend for a while, had previously lived in Cambridge, Massachusetts, had worked in a psychiatric hospital in Boston, was thirty-seven years old, and had held twenty-five jobs. He liked to have a six-pack of cheap beer at the end the day.

To these facts I added all sorts of bits and pieces about who I *thought* he was. I thought he was a charming New England intellectual, brilliant, worldly, and sophisticated. I was fascinated by him. I thought he had fabulous ideas that put mine to shame. He was deep, he was exotic; I was simple and plain and unexciting. I thought he was wonderful and I was not. He couldn't possibly like me for who I was.

I became very attached to these illusions and to my desire to have him like me, nevertheless. In so doing, I created a sort of hell for my self that went on for years.

The insecurities and self-doubt I put my self through during the first years of our relationship were awful. I remember consciously asking my self, "Would he like me if I looked like that?" "Would he think I was more interesting if I was like her?" I was constantly searching for what I could do to be appealing and interesting to him. I was sure I was not.

Small fights with him would devastate me. I would feel lost, fearful that our relationship was over; I would feel the bottom dropping out from under me. I became agitated and unable to concentrate. Things that generally brought me pleasure became unimportant and were cast aside. I would pursue arguments for hours, hoping we could come to some point where I again felt sure I wasn't losing him. Without my awareness, I had lost my self in my pursuit to not lose him.

What I was also not aware of was that this man had his own issues with work and relationships and, as I've hinted, alcohol. I had finally found the rebellious sort I'd sought out in the seventh grade. But this one was cloaked in intellect and social class, which made our being together seem more appropriate and okay. He appeared hardly available to me emotionally, and this drew me like a magnet.

Fortunately, some relief for my lostness presented itself in the form of a book and counseling. Walking through the mall one day, I spotted a recently released book entitled *Women Who Love Too Much: When You Keep Wishing and Hoping He'll Change.* I was intrigued. The title alone resonated for me, and still does to this day. I got it, read it, and participated in a study group on the book. It was the beginning of the way out at last, the way out of my lostness, anxiety, and despair. I was starting to see some of my dynamics relative to caretaking, managing and controlling, and hoping to change someone else. Still scared to death that my relationship with this man would end, I was fragile—more informed, but fragile.

I had entered counseling to help me with these same issues. I was feeling so bad in this relationship that I'd been to see a psychologist for the first time in my life. I did this also because I thought this man, my live-in partner, would like me to do it. He did.

The counseling was pleasant, comforting, and somewhat revealing, but our work didn't help me with my entanglements with my partner. I don't think I shared the true depth of these issues with this male psychotherapist. I was too ashamed. It didn't help that my therapist moved to another state before we'd finished our work. Nor did it help that the issue of alcoholism was never raised. Insight I had gained, but my pain remained.

Through *Women Who Love Too Much,* and this first venture into counseling, I began to sense that the way out of my entanglements involved getting my focus on my self and not on the other person. But this was only a start. Years of learning to disentangle were ahead of me.

Somewhere around this time, I made a decision that was both healthy and unhealthy. I applied and was accepted into a PhD program in psychology. Likely I was trying to gain some self-esteem. I am a good student, and without much awareness I was seeking the good feelings that come from academic successes. I certainly was not feeling these things in my primary relationship.

After some serious conversations with my self, and the welcoming psychology department, I chose to decline this wonderful opportunity for two reasons. The healthy reason, or so it seemed to me, was that I was good at school and lousy at relationships. I decided that rather than run away from this relationship, I would stay and work on it and me.

The other reason was the unhealthy one: I feared that if I went away to graduate school I would lose this man, and I couldn't bear the thought. It felt like a great risk that my abandonment fears could not tolerate. So I said, "No thank you."

I have not regretted that decision. I have in fact stayed the course, choosing to work on my intimacy difficulties and increase my capacity for a healthy relationship. Consider this book my dissertation, a document that captures the experience, strength, and hope I've gathered through the educational path I chose.

In September 1987, we were married in a service on the front lawn of our home, with our friends and my family present. In August 1988, our most wonderful daughter was born. In November of that same year my husband entered treatment. His diagnosis: alcoholism.

Finally, we had a name, a label, a way to conceptualize the craziness we'd been living with. We both took it seriously and embarked on our paths to recovery.

I started attending Al-Anon meetings right away, though not particularly for the right reasons. I saw the meetings as interesting and fun. I enjoyed hearing people's stories and intellectually absorbing the steps and traditions of the program, but for a while I did not bring my emotional pain with me. I temporarily felt better. My husband's diagnosis and treatment gave me some relief, with the understanding that the awfulness I had been experiencing was not all me. That was good to know. For a while, I lost touch with my insanity. Now that I knew he had been insane, I felt quite sane.

Thank heavens I continued to go to meetings because it wasn't long before my insanity was back. In my periodic journal I wrote:

> *"I feel depressed . . . a feeling of dread . . . a feeling that I have/am doing something very wrong."*

> *"I am consumed by my disease. I am anxious and depressed and my thinking is obsessive . . . I am trying to lay low and hang with my Higher Power. Every which way I turn my thoughts are catastrophic."*

My husband's recovery was vital, but it did not cure my insecurities, abandonment fears, or anxieties. It did not result in excellent communication between us, improvement in our ability to work together, or comfort with intimacy. All of those energy-sapping difficulties were still there.

We each had identified people and resources we could use to help us. My twelve-step program became a major influence for me.

In one of my twelve-step meetings a member said, "My therapist does not like for me to come to these meetings. He says they brainwash you. But you know, I think my brain needed washing." Yes, my brain needed washing as well. The ways I thought about my self and relationships and how to get what I thought I wanted, all needed remaking. I needed to learn to think about me and not the other person so much. I needed to learn when I was forcing solutions and to stop doing that. I needed to learn what I could and could not control, to quit doing the same thing expecting different results. I needed to cultivate my spirituality. And the rethinking goes on and on.

I have been on this path for three decades. I have had the help of many excellent members from my twelve-step fellowship, an incredible sponsor, and several good and knowing friends outside the program. They have offered me inspiring thoughts to help guide me to new places:

"One person drinks and the rest of us go crazy."

"I abandon my self."

"Be careful about forcing solutions."

"What I need to know will come to my attention without any effort on my part."

"We keep the focus on ourselves."

"The evidence that my higher power is going before me is so strong."

I also had the help of a wonderful, experienced therapist and mentor with a deep understanding of the issue of losing your self to another. She offered me insight after insight about my self and ways to find and keep my self. My journal is full of concise, to-the-point statements she made to help me with this rethinking:

"You have not succeeded in pleasing him so far. You are not going to please him. So please you."

"Just act like a person would. You don't have to get permission."

"Find the truth in whatever ways you can."

"Letting go is scary as hell, because it involves a leap of faith."

The Third Twenty-or-So Years

Disentangle started in the mid-1990s when I was in my early forties. It grew out of the personal work of mine that had found its way into my professional work with clients. Al-Anon, counseling and daily practices all helped. Over twenty years later, *Disentangle* remains rooted in this personal and professional work, though it has been enriched tremendously by recent developments in evidence-based practices and a deeper understanding of complex topics such as trauma, attachment theory, and neuroscience.

This book is about finding and cultivating your self. My working understanding of codependency is that its central feature is a loss of self. Until the fields of mental health and addiction establish an agreed-upon definition of codependency, I will continue to focus on this development of a healthy self. Whether or not we are ready to call this loss of self "codependency" is irrelevant. Loss of self is loss of self. It has its own consequences and merits treatment, whatever we decide to call it.

I have had many opportunities to teach the material in this book and to update it with current research data that supports the tools we are using. Questions posed by participants in workshops, retreats, and conference presentations have often invited me to explore the material more deeply and to expand on what can be helpful in our recovery.

My family is intact. My husband and I are together, working our programs on a daily basis. Our daughter lives in Boston and works successfully as a freelance artist. My stepdaughter lives in Memphis and is happily employed. Both daughters are in satisfying relationships. My mother and my father are deceased. My brother lives in Richmond, Virginia, and tends to the family properties. We are all in good communication and glad when we get to see each other.

I continue to study and use what I have learned through my twelve-step fellowship. Some of my closest friends are people I met through that fellowship, and speaking with these people-in-the-know continues to be both comforting and helpful as we work to practice the fellowship's principles in all our affairs.

My daily practices keep me on my recovery track, which gives me strength and serenity. These daily practices include readings, connecting with my breath, stretching my body, pausing before reacting, appreciating silence, acting in ways that protect my serenity, knowing what to let go of, knowing when to stop, and connecting with my spirituality. My daily practices also include the basics: healthy eating, getting enough sleep, and regular exercise.

Every day *ain't* great, as I've been known to point out. Life is challenging in ways both big and small. We are continual works in progress. I know that today I am much quieter, more still, and less afraid. I can naturally pause, consider, and take in. I know and can be with my feelings. I can speak up, listen, and clarify. Maybe aging has helped me with all of this. I feel wiser and more centered. I feel less reactive and bask in many a moment through the day. I believe this growth is not just from aging, however. My work with disentangling has helped me to change in these ways as well.

Things are not perfect in my life. I can still lose my self in someone else. I can still fall into being the main caregiver, provider, and the make-things-happen person. I can feel on the outside of relationships and life—inadequate, incompetent, or soon to be abandoned. And I can lose my self in other things, such as work, worry, and shopping. I can overwork and exhaust myself. I can be upset and have trouble letting something go. I can question decisions I have made; I can doubt myself. I can go buy things I don't need, when I really should just go home and rest.

My sense of self and my love and care for my self have grown tremendously. I have a healthy connection with my self, even if that connection gets interrupted or is not strong or clear at times. When that happens, I know what to do—I use what I am teaching in this book. I know that self is the place for me to come back to for serenity and strength, the place that cannot be taken from me, the place that anchors me and helps me not to lose my self in someone or something.

I prefer to live in the now. I am much more well-defined by me. And it has become almost second nature for me to "Quietly Be.

Quietly See," as I wrote about at the conclusion of the first edition of this book:

Quietly Be. Quietly See.

Over and over, I catch my self about to say or do something to force a solution.

Some years ago, I was trying to create a conversation with my husband. There was no problem afoot as far as I was aware, so it wasn't like I was trying to make things okay again between us (like I can do that anyway). We were just hanging out in front of the television at the end of the day. Consciously or unconsciously, I had decided I wanted some contact with him. So I started asking mundane questions, which he politely answered with one-word responses. I could feel my self getting irritated at his not joining me in the ways I would have liked, so I applied some detachment and excused my self to bed with a not-so-great spirit.

The next morning as I drove to work, I was thinking about the previous evening and realized how I'd been trying to make things the way I wanted them to be. I wanted my husband to show interest in me and my day. I wanted him to pay attention to me and not to the television. I wanted to know he was glad to see me. I wanted some contact with him. I could not make any of this happen. It was not in my control, and I had set my self up by having these hopes and expectations.

It then came to me that I need to "quietly be."

Now you'd think I would have this down pat by now, but I don't.

Quietly be.

That's a nice thought. I wrote it down on a slip of paper and have kept it close ever since.

Quietly be. Just sit. Be present. Be present with my self and the situation. Allow life to flow. Perhaps a conversation will come. Perhaps I will just enjoy being, and being in the presence of someone else. Whatever I seek may already be. Whatever I need is probably already there. Quietly be, Nancy, with what is.

Several weeks later, as I woke from my night's sleep, the phrase "quietly see" came to me. I knew right away that this was the second piece. As I quietly be, I become aware of all sorts of things, good and bad, pleasing and disturbing. I don't need to judge them, but simply to see them and experience them.

Quietly see.

How different this is than being entangled and trying to force solutions! When I am doing those things, I can't or won't see things as they are. In fact, my very entangled behaviors are efforts not to experience and see things as they are, but to make them as I believe they should be.

So now I "quietly be and quietly see." And in so doing, I open my self to the spiritual realm of life. Forcing things is just me acting like I know what's best for me and others. When I let this forcing go, I let go to my higher power with excitement and eager anticipation about how things are now and what is to come.

Who knows what the next twenty-or-so years have in store for me?

3 AS WE EMBARK

Over the last twenty years, I've learned a great deal. Through my preparation for workshops and retreats, as well as continuing education for myself, I have acquired both new information and a better understanding of this process of untangling and its application to other areas of our lives. One process area I have become clearer about is what it takes to change.

Stages of Change

But first some context. The field of treatment today recognizes six Stages of Change, as identified by Prochaska and DiClemente. Understanding that change is a process is crucial, and knowing which stage you are in can help greatly moving forward.

- **Precontemplation:** You have no plans to change and may not even be aware that a problem exists.

- **Contemplation:** You are aware there is a problem and are considering making a change, but not immediately.

- **Preparation:** You are ready to make a change in the near future. You believe the change is good and believe you can make this change. You do things to get ready for the change, including learning skills, gathering social support, and preparing for obstacles.

- **Action:** You are practicing new behaviors. This is an active process of changing behaviors with social support, believing in your ability to make these changes even when you run into obstacles, and working through the feelings of loss that may come with the changes you are making. Remembering the long-term benefits of these changes is of great benefit in reinforcing your efforts.

- **Maintenance:** You continue to make the changes you desire, and new behaviors replace old ones. You maintain these changes through social support and reinforcement of internal rewards (e.g., feeling happier, more serenity, less conflict). You develop coping strategies in case of a relapse to the problem behaviors.

- **Relapse:** You return to your old, problematic behaviors. At this point, you evaluate what triggered the relapse, assess your motivation to resume the changes you had made, and fortify your coping behaviors to prevent another relapse.

Depending on each individual's progress, these stages can repeat themselves. Hopefully the individual learns from each progression through these stages, and relapses to old behaviors become less frequent while new behaviors become more firmly established, the individual increasingly commits to their changes and to the benefits they experience.

Ingredients of Change

As we move through these stages, aspects of our self, our motivations, our attitudes, and our beliefs make substantial differences in our ability to make the changes we say we would like to make.

Change involves much more than simply saying that's what we are going to do—though we often wish otherwise. Hopeful wishes and magic wands, even good intentions, are appealing, but can carry us only so far. Working with my self and others, I have developed a list of ten ingredients I believe are essential as we embark on change. This information is about change for our self, not about changing someone else. We can say we want to change our self, but without these deep and personal ingredients, our progress will be slow, frustrating, sometimes altogether stuck.

When stuck in the process, I have found it useful to consider these ingredients and see where I may be lacking. Then I know where I need to do my work, in order to ultimately keep moving forward.

1. **Awareness.** Awareness is everything. Without it we cannot change. If we are not aware of our self, we are not aware of our own part in the problems we may be experiencing, and thus cannot possibly know what we need to change. This is the precontemplative stage. Recovery entails bringing many things into our awareness and being willing to maintain this level of awareness as we continue to make changes. Awareness means noticing our body and our health, our behaviors and their consequences, and our moods, which may involve tone of voice, internal energy, and motivations as we express our self. Awareness also includes noticing how things are for us in our home, our social life, and our occupation. Awareness opens the door to what we may

want to change, then supports and guides us as we make those changes.

2. **Willingness.** Willingness is just as essential to change as awareness. We can be aware of our self and the changes we want to make on our own behalf, yet have no willingness to act on these things. It is vital that we assess our willingness to do whatever it takes to make these changes. Assessing can help us to see that though we want the outcome of the changes we seek, we are only 50 percent willing to do the things needed. That, then, is the place for us to do our work. What has us only 50 percent willing? What is blocking us? What would help to increase our willingness? This is why change can be so difficult. We may be quite clear on how we want to be, but the deeper work required can arouse our fears, resistances, even self-protections that may no longer be needed. As we meet these challenges, we do well to consider our willingness to work through those things that hold us in place and keep us from acting, thinking, and feeling in new ways.

3. **Intentionality.** Being intentional means that we are maintaining our awareness and making conscious decisions about how we want to act and what we want to do. Change does not happen just because we desire it, even in the very depth of our being. Change happens when we are willing to work on it, and when we add intentionality to the mix, so that we speak, act, and make choices consistent with what we want to change.

4. **Self-Education.** Once we have become aware, willing, and intentional about the changes we wish to make, self-education is often needed. All of a sudden we have a new word for what we may be dealing with: anxiety,

depression, alcoholism, codependency. This issue may have remained unnamed until now, and we may find we know very little about it. Reading about and studying what we are dealing with is important. Things that seemed like random symptoms become part of a more complete picture. What you have been feeling and experiencing begins to make more sense to you as you learn. This self-education extends to learning ways to address these issues, so you can make healthy changes. These may include counseling, support groups, inpatient treatment, skill-building, medications, and daily readings. Additionally, as we self-educate, we wonder what it will be like for us to make these changes: Will this be hard for me? What else in my life may change as a result? What else in me may change?

5. **Skill-Building.** Learning new skills naturally follows from awareness, willingness, intentionality, and self-education. Although we may know what we are ready to work on for change, it's likely we do not have all the skills to make it happen. If money management is our problem, we may have to learn how to budget. If we have disordered eating, we may have to learn what healthy meals and snacks look like. If we have trouble saying "no," we may have to learn assertiveness. If we are chronically anxious, we may have to learn how to calm our self. Change requires all sorts of new skills and tools. Some of them we may have learned earlier in life and chosen not to use on a regular basis; others we may never have been taught. It's funny how many life-enhancing skills we never learn until we really need them. Now that you really need them, prepare to skill-build.

6. **Self-Regard.** To be able to stay on our healing path, it's beneficial to maintain our self-regard as we work toward change. This means that we care enough about our self to ensure that we consider our self and our interests as we move through the day. It means keeping our self front and center as we make decisions about how to spend our time and resources. This does not mean we are selfish; rather, that we are able to keep a balance in care for self and care for others. It means we intentionally put our self in the formula as plans and decisions are made. What would be best for you? How could that fit with what you need to do for you? We do this not just because we are, in fact, a variable in the equation, but also because we care about our self. We have a warm regard for our self, and we want to remember that and tend to it.

7. **Noticing Self in the Moment.** This is an extension of awareness. "Noticing" is a word often used in mindfulness practices. We notice the taste of our food, the sound of a bell, the feel of the breeze. In this case, noticing is being aware of our words, tone, actions, thoughts, and impulses as they are happening in the present moment. It is this level of self-awareness that will enable us to catch our self in habitual responses and old ways of being, creating the possibility in that moment to do or say something different, something more consistent with the changes we want to make. Or we may notice our self in the present moment and find that we are in fact changing, that we have succeeded in managing an impulse or asserting our self in a constructive way. Noticing our self in both ways is of equal importance, and letting that positivity seep in thoroughly will help to reinforce our changes, literally reprogramming us neurologically in the direction of confidence and health.

8. **Intervening on Our Own Behalf.** Noticing our self in the present moment can look like this: "Here I am again. I can say and do the same old thing or, in this moment, I can do something different." Intervening on our own behalf is doing something different in that moment. In that moment, we have the choice of the same old, same old, or we can instead use new skills to handle the situation in the direction of our desired changes. We can be coached and advised, but in that moment, we are the agent of our own change.

9. **Spirituality.** Though we are the only one who can make the changes we want in our self, this work is best done in connection with our spiritual self. We are not all-powerful; there are limits to what we can and cannot do. Many things we just do not know. Sometimes things don't work out the way we had hoped or intended. Other times we are amazed at what has happened for the good, well beyond what we might have expected. All of this speaks to the importance of our spiritual development, in whatever form that may take: a higher power, something bigger than our self, something beyond our understanding, God, Love, or Soul. As we change our self, connecting with our source of spirituality deeply enhances our comfort and wisdom—wisdom to know what and how we can change, and wisdom to know when we would do best to let go.

10. **Letting Go.** As much as it concerns acquiring and adding, change also requires letting go. In making changes, we acquire new skills, new routines, new possessions, new points of view, new attitudes, new friends, new places, and new ideas. As we make these positive shifts in our lives, however, we find letting go necessary as

well, in order to bring in the new. New attitudes and ideas may require letting go of former beliefs. New skills and routines may mean letting go of old habits. We may also have to let go of hopes, dreams, people, and our expectations of others. Knowing that letting go is an ingredient of change is especially critical in those moments when you start to realize that holding on is no longer working for you.

On Being Resilient

Resilience is the ability to rebound from adversity, trauma, or major life stressors with family, relationships, money, or work. It is our ability to learn and grow, even though we may have experienced difficult, even harmful, events and people in our lives. Resilience can be developed; it is not an inborn trait. The skills that promote resilience are consistent with the ingredients of change and the foundational concepts of disentangling. In fact, they are rooted in connecting with and actualizing our self for recovery. "The Road to Resilience," an excellent brochure from the American Psychological Association, has informed the following brief look at some of the resilience-building skills that will prepare us further as we embark on our journey to a healthy self.

- **Internal locus of control.** Internal locus of control is a psychological concept developed by Julian Rotter in the 1950s. The individual with an internal locus of control believes that they have within their self the abilities and skills to succeed, whereas the individual with an external locus of control perceives their life as being controlled by fate, luck, or powers outside of them. Though neither of these orientations is necessarily good or bad, research has shown that people with an internal locus of control are more successful, less stress-driven, and handle strong emotions effectively.

Resilience means accessing and developing this internal locus of control. In so doing, one is able to cultivate a set of beliefs that fosters the perception of tragic events as surmountable. They believe they can recover from what has happened to them, seeing their self in a positive light, with confidence in their ability to grow from this adversity.

As an extension of these positive, forward-moving beliefs, the resilient individual comes to accept that changes happen in life, and they are able to focus on what they can change and control in light of the adversity they have experienced. They are able to set realistic goals for themselves, remaining hopeful and ready to take action.

• **Self-Development.** It's clear that resilience calls for the development of self. With a healthy internal locus of control, the resilient individual embarks on an assortment of things that promote self-growth: reading, studying, learning, identifying personal strengths, trying new things, meeting new people, and being willing to see things from different points of view. These activities help the individual to understand their self, their experiences, and their situation better, and to see what they can learn from the trauma and major stressors they've experienced.

Self-care is an important aspect of resilience as well. As the individual does this work for self-growth, care of self is essential. A good night's sleep, healthy meals, and regular exercise promote the healthy self we are seeking. Keeping up with medical and dental concerns, as well as appointments for massages, haircuts, and other services that promote health and good feelings, makes a world of difference in our overall outlook.

- **Skills Development.** This self-growth and forward movement requires the learning of new skills. Communication skills are at the top of that list—learning to express self in assertive ways is essential. Trauma can leave an individual feeling powerless in their life. Helping the individual to understand not only what they can control, but also how to express what they do want and need, helps with resilience. Other valuable communication skills include active listening and conflict resolution. Additionally, problem-solving skills help the individual to think through a problem, identify the outcome they wish for, name steps to reach that outcome, examine in advance the consequences of these steps, decide on their plan, and take action.

  Healthy emotional management skills can also be learned. Many of us don't know how to handle strong emotions. Throw in a major life difficulty, and we know even less what to do with our anger, distress, worry, outrage, sadness, or bafflement. Learning to identify and name our feelings is the beginning. Then we learn what we can do with those feelings and how to express them in respectful, constructive, and effective ways.

- **Support Development.** Cultivating resilience involves finding sources of support for self. Support can come from family, friends, and professionals who understand the depths of the adversity experienced by the individual and are thus good listeners. Specific support groups may also provide such understanding, comfort, and presence. Books and online resources can provide support. Such materials may offer education, as well as stories about people who

have experienced similar traumas and managed to find
their way through.

Spirituality can be yet another resource for support.
Though becoming resilient is about developing an internal
locus of control, this does not mean the individual has full
control over everything. Learning to discern what we do
and do not have control over, and being able to let go of
the things we cannot control or fix, is essential to resilience.
Believing that we *can* let go of such things, to something
larger than our self, can be very helpful, supportive, and
freeing.

And So

Whether it is adversity, trauma, or difficult stressors with family,
relationships, money, and work that has brought you to this book,
it's clear that our recovery path—which incorporates resilience—
is about bringing a healthy focus to our self with awareness,
willingness, a readiness to learn new things, an intention to bring
them actively into our lives, and the confidence that we can do
this for our self.

"In a way I'm glad I'm out of there."

"I feel like I'm coming out of
the twilight zone."

"Unbelievable; I have been so
wrapped up in one individual."

UNTANGLING

as shared by various people along the way

"I can stay in my marriage
and be my self."

"It's just good common sense."

4 THE BIG PICTURE

The seeds of this book were planted one day in the mid-1990s, when at the end of a counseling session, a client said to me, "I understand what you mean about 'detaching,' but how do you *do* that?" What an excellent question!

I had experienced entanglements for quite some time, but recently the fundamental pieces of how to untangle my self had started to come together. I'd been gathering these ideas in random ways over the years, but my work with clients required me to get down to nuts and bolts in a more organized way to help us find our self again and increase peace and serenity in our lives.

The themes of entanglement issues rooted in loss of self were clear:

"What is wrong with me?"

"Am I doing something wrong?"

"Who am I separate from this other person?"

"Do I know who I am?"

"Do I know what I think? feel? know? believe? want?"

"If I back off, will they leave me?"

"If I back off, will they survive?"

"If I back off, will I survive?"

"How much of the problem is me?"

"What should I do about their problem?"

"What should I do about my problem?"

"How much do I want to put up with?"

"What do I do when I've had enough?"

"Suppose I don't know if I've had enough?"

"What do you mean, 'What do I want?'"

"What do you mean, 'What's good for me?'"

We are encouraged to use many tools for good mental health—speak up, say no, listen, let go—but how *do* we do those things? Each tool requires self-understanding and a number of skills in order to use it effectively.

My client's question prompted me to compose a quick list of ideas that reflected input from counseling theories and techniques as well as twelve-step wisdom. It also included ideas drawn from my own experience, strength, and hope. I realized that many of my clients were dealing with entanglement issues. Whether it was a difficult boss, an overbearing in-law, an unfaithful partner, or an oppositional child, the entangled person experienced a loss of self in the other person and thus an inability to know what to do to make positive changes.

I drafted an organized list of these ideas. Over time this list has evolved, and is still a work in progress, always organic, always open to new ideas and subject to revision. As I move along on this journey, I continue to see old things in new ways, to see how what I perceive and understand today may be altered by a new insight tomorrow.

Even though this list of ideas is subject to constant revision, to allow for increased depth in our work, it has remained essentially the same at its core. The core consists of four areas of work: Facing Illusions, Detaching, Setting Healthy Boundaries, and Spirituality. These four areas are not meant to be addressed in any particular order. Thus, I prefer to present them in a circle, as we are always working on each and every one of them. Yes, we make progress, very good progress, but this is not a checklist where I can address one area then say I am done with it. We may be using skills in one area, find our self still stuck, and realize we would do well to add skills from another area. This work with our self becomes part of our daily life with our ever-evolving awareness, understanding, and skill development.

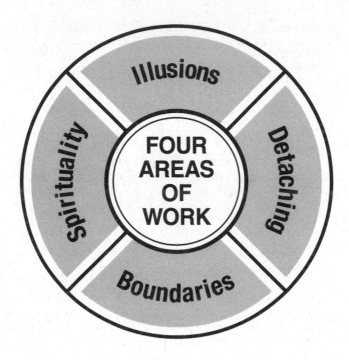

This circular illustration indicates the four areas of work addressed in this book, as well as their dynamic interplay. These may be read in a circular way, but we can also move across the circle from one skill area to another, for example, realizing that we are Detaching but have completely lost contact with our Spirituality. Or we could be doing well with our Spirituality, but find our self neglecting our Boundaries. I like to think of these four development areas as road signs for us as we cultivate our healthy self. When we start to feel lost, it's useful to notice the signs—Illusions, Detaching, Boundaries, and Spirituality—and remember the specific skills we have learned, and the direction those skills can take us.

Here is an overview of those skill sets as they appear in the list I originally drafted.

IDEAS FOR DISENTANGLING

Facing Illusions

- Find *the truth* about you, the other person, and your situation.

- Work with your self to accept the truth you find.

Detaching

- Become aware of who and what *entangles* you.

- Learn to separate your problem from the other person's problem.

- Don't try to fix their problem.

- Find your emotional balance:

    - *Observe* the other person more than fully interact with them.

    - *Respond* rather than *react*.

    - Use *self-talk*.

- Be aware of the *motivations* behind what you say and do in interacting with the other person.

Setting Healthy Boundaries

- Slow down.

- Listen and respond to your own needs, wants, limits, beliefs, and feelings.

- Use "I" statements.

- Make "I" statements rather than ask questions.

- Set and state your boundaries.

- Stick with your boundaries.

- Say things once.

- Say things cleanly and without extensive discussion.

- Stick to the topic.

- Stay in the present.

- Listen to the other person.

- Try not to defend, rationalize, explain, justify, or convince the other person.

- Be aware and observant of your emotions and behaviors as you express them.

- Learn when to stop.

- Stop.

Developing Spirituality

- Slow down.

- Simplify.

- Be in the present.

- Find some solitude.

- Breathe deeply.

- Relax your body.

- Quiet your mind.

- Sit in silence.

- Discover your higher power.

- Have an ongoing relationship with your higher power.

- Let go of things you cannot control.

- Practice these things.

- Cultivate faith.

This overview captures the big picture of disentangling. Collectively, these ideas give us power, confidence, serenity, and hope for our self. Our habitual ways have had us focusing on the needs of others, evaluating our self through the eyes of others, and generally lacking a useful connection with our self. As we work on shifting our focus to self in healthy ways, we have to learn new skills. It is not uncommon in my work to find that when a person usually busy doing things for others has some time alone, they don't know what to do with their self.

The shift to an internal focus is essential. But we do not magically know what to do, even when we have gently turned our heads to look in our own direction. What do we do with the uncomfortable feelings that arise, with the pressure we feel to be as we usually are, with the holes left in our day and in our sense of self? New skills are part of what will help us manage and answer these questions.

I offer this list to clients in individual and group therapy. I offer it to individuals as I see the value in their working on these elements. I am amazed at how often I share this information. Certainly, clients coming in for help with family members and friends suffering from addiction frequently benefit by work in this area—other clients may be less clear about needing this information at first.

A client of mine came in for panic attacks and anxiety. The panic was interfering with his daily functioning, he was missing his construction work for fear of an attack, and he had ulcers and periodic rashes. As I got to know him, he shared concerns about his relationship with his wife, who'd had several affairs. She did not want to commit to him, but did not want to leave either. It quickly became clear how entangled he was in their relationship, absolutely stuck about what to do next.

A woman came to see me, concerned about her anger toward her young children, and wanted to learn to manage her feelings and behaviors with them. I learned the history of a harsh and controlling childhood with the grandparents who had raised her. Her anger with her grandfather was still very strong. She readily reexperienced his teasing, criticism, and sexual harassment of her. She was furious with him. She was angry with her children, one of whom reminded her of her grandfather. She could hardly contain her self.

Client by client, as I see the need, I pull out this handout of "Ideas for Disentangling," copy it again, and we begin the work. I am often struck by how similar their issues and feelings are despite the differences in their stories.

The following chapters will take this overview of disentangling and examine in greater detail the components of it, which have become clearer as we have worked and lived with these ideas.

First we will look at what I call *The Basics*. *The Basics* are general descriptions of what disentangling is about. *The Basics* are intended to help you understand what this process involves and what it can offer you.

Then we will explore *The Four Areas of Work* central to disentangling, looking at each of the "Ideas for Disentangling" presented above. We will consider what each idea means, evaluate the reasons for its usefulness, and think about practical ways to apply it.

5 THE BASICS

Clients coming to psychotherapy for the first time often have no idea what to expect. They imagine it will be like a doctor's appointment, where they describe their symptoms, the doctor writes them a prescription, and the problem is taken care of with one visit. Sometimes they ask questions about how long the therapy may take or if their therapy will help them to change another person in their life. They are unfamiliar with our ethics of confidentiality, sanctions against dual relationships, and the professional boundaries we must employ with people who sometimes want us to also be their friend. They need my professional guidance on these process issues.

Similarly, the process of disentangling merits an explanation. It might best be described in terms of what it is about and what it is not.

Some people identify immediately with the word "disentangle." The expression on their face and the glimmer in their eyes tells me they know right away and just might sense the need for untangling from somebody or something. It strikes a familiar chord.

It is not uncommon, however, for people who are attached to somebody or something to experience anxiety and skepticism when I describe this process. Their abandonment issues come right to the surface. They fear I am talking about separation, about divorce, about being alone and empty forever.

Then there are those who think that to disentangle would be selfish. What will happen to the other person if they don't take care of them? Wouldn't it be wrong not to help or take care of them? At the thought of saying or doing things to take care of their self, guilt comes pouring forth.

And then there is the reaction of the person who tells me they simply have no idea what I'm talking about when I suggest they take a look at their self first. *They* are not the one with the problem. They've come to me to get help for the other person. They are confused by the idea of disentangling, may even feel put off by it, believing that I'm not responding to the real issues that brought them to therapy.

The following ten descriptions explain what I mean when I talk about disentangling as a process. This information can help you to understand what this process is all about and what it can offer you, as well as your part in it.

THE BASICS
It's about Losing Your Self

Entanglement is being consumed with worry, care, thoughts, anxieties, plans, regrets, anger, frustration, confusion, exhilaration, anticipation, fantasies, hopes, and dreams about another person. It is feeling lost, not knowing what to do next, feeling hardly able to take care of what needs to be done. Entanglement is fear, dark expectations, and impending doom. It is a high that feels absolutely great, that you seek again and again. Entanglement is having little to no awareness of you and what you need; it is the experience of not being aware that you are not in touch with you.

Disentangling is about recognizing that you have lost your self in someone else.

I have found this experience of loss of self to be common among people, whether they identify as codependent, adult children of addicts, or people who love too much. The clinical issues are often similar, if not the same. Though the specifics of their situations may differ, they are each entangled with other people and sacrificing their self as a result.

Codependence has not yet achieved a single agreed-upon definition, but the common definitions all reflect this loss of self.

Co-Dependents Anonymous (CoDA) suggests that people look at their patterns and characteristics of denial, low self-esteem, control, compliance, and avoidance, to determine whether they might benefit from their participation in CoDA.

In *Codependent No More*, Melody Beattie describes codependence as letting our self be affected by another person's behavior and being obsessed with trying to control that other person's behavior.

Timmen L. Cermak, applying the clinical model of the *Diagnostic and Statistical Manual of Mental Disorders (DSM-5)*, defines codependence as a pattern of personality traits that define our self-esteem by our ability to influence or control the feelings and behaviors of someone else and our assumption of responsibility for meeting the needs of others to the exclusion of our own.

The subtitle to Robin Norwood's *Women Who Love Too Much* is "When You Keeping Wishing and Hoping He'll Change." She describes loving too much as a process that encompasses low self-esteem, a need to be needed, a strong urge to change and control others, and a willingness to suffer.

Some of these definitions were included in the 2005 research project Dear, Roberts, and Lange conducted in which they studied eleven of the most commonly used definitions of codependence. Through a statistical analysis of these definitions, they found four defining features of codependency: external focusing, self-sacrificing, interpersonal control, and emotional suppression.

In my most recent work, I describe the codependent as over-functioning in someone else's life and under-functioning in their own life. This means that the codependent is taking care of, responding to, worrying about, trying to fix, or trying to please someone else to a greater extent than they are for their self.

They are, in other words, letting the life of someone else eclipse their own to a damaging extent. I want to emphasize this "damaging extent"; it's a necessary distinction. Many behaviors we associate with codependency are not problematic in and of themselves: taking care of, helping, serving, fixing, pleasing. They become problematic when we go too far with them, letting our lives and the lives of others be dominated by these behaviors, to the neglect of self.

Some questions to illustrate this over-functioning for others and under-functioning for self:

- Do you do for others what they could do for themselves (e.g., homework, phone calls, bill paying, cooking, etc.)?

- Do you make sure everything is taken care of for someone else without giving a thought to what you need?

- Do you postpone what you were going to do for you in order to do what others want you to do?

- Do you feel pressure to say "yes" to the nonurgent requests of others?

- Do you have no clue what you feel, need, or want to do when given the opportunity to pay attention to you?

Another way I describe codependency is by looking at the word itself. The term "codependent" was originally coined to describe the relationship between the alcoholic and the person actively involved in their care and management. Of particular importance is the "co" part of the word; it means we are in this together. I would suggest that the "co" part of this dependency works like this: First, the person for whom the codependent is over-functioning is *dependent* on the codependent for all that they do to keep everyone's head above water, while the codependent is *dependent* on being needed by the other person. This is the codependent deal. Second, because the codependent has built their life around this other person, their own sense of self is *dependent* on things external, including how this other person is doing, how this other person is treating them, what this other person is telling them about their self, etc.

Here are some further questions to illustrate this dependence on being needed and this dependence on things outside our self to define our sense of self:

- Do you prefer to reach out to help someone else before you take care of your self?

- Do you feel a rise in energy and engagement when helping others?

- Do you fill the empty spaces in your life by focusing on other people?

- Do you worry a lot about people over whom you have no control?

- Do you feel lost when no one needs you to do something?

Each of these definitions of codependence can be useful, as they all speak to real people with real interpersonal dynamics that lead to real problems. I have found it helpful, though, to see that at the core of all of these definitions is the experience of loss of self, and my clients have found this a useful way to work with their problems. We don't have to decide whether they are codependent or not. Some clients resist this description, or what they think this description means; we don't have to get hung up on it. Sometimes their entanglements do not exhibit controlling, compliance, or caretaking behaviors. We don't have to find the addiction in their family history, or the person they are trying to change. We only have to get in touch with their experience of losing their self in another and the insanity that can follow.

Entanglement is losing your self in someone else. Responses to that entanglement vary quite a bit. You may want to control the other person, fix them, or change them. You may want to simply be with them no matter what. You may be willing to change your self so that you can be with them. Regardless of the nature of your response to the entanglement, the process of disentangling is about your lost self and about how to retrieve *you* from that tangled mess.

THE BASICS
It's about Unhealthy Attachments

It is normal to want things. It is normal to desire love and companionship, to get attached to things and people that mean a lot to us, and to care about others and wish them well. It is normal to extend our self to other people or to causes we may take on. These things enrich our lives, give them increased depth and meaning, and help us understand our self better. These are healthy attachments.

Disentangling is about attachments that have become unhealthy.

The *DSM-5* is the principal reference for diagnosing mental health problems. One of the criteria the *DSM-5* uses for many of the disorders included is that the condition must cause significant distress or problems in major areas of life functioning, such as relationships, work, school, and health. I find this concept useful not only in defining the diagnosable clinical problems of my clients, but also in looking at this idea of unhealthy attachments.

Unhealthy attachments can cause significant problems in our social or occupational functioning. An unhealthy attachment to another person may cause us to:

- Not go to work or school.
- Fail to be prepared for work or school.
- Neglect our children.
- Neglect our health.
- Neglect our responsibilities.
- Misspend our money.
- Hide in bed all day or all week.
- Contract a sexually transmitted disease.
- Get arrested.
- Lie.
- Steal.
- Cheat.
- Lose our job.

- Lose our temper.

- Lose our friends.

- Lose our family.

- Lose our mind.

Unhealthy attachments can cause us to lose track of what's important to us. They preoccupy our thoughts, and they preoccupy our behaviors as well. We pursue, snoop, sneak, watch, and wait. We wait and wait, for things to be better, for things to be more like we'd like them to be, while the rest of our life goes to hell. And we don't even care. We may not even notice. It just doesn't seem to matter.

All that matters is this person to whom we have become attached. All our thoughts and behaviors are riveted on this person, on their thoughts and behaviors. Our focus has become so narrow that this is all we see. We have blinders on to the other parts of our life and, ironically, the reality of our relationship with this other person. We are so up in their face we cannot see clearly, and as a result, our daily functioning with other people, with work, and with care of our self is shot.

We have developed an unhealthy attachment.

THE BASICS
It's about Finding You

The process of disentangling is about retrieving our self from the tangled web in which we're caught. It's about removing the threads (or ropes!) that have us bound to this unhealthy attachment. Then, once we have some freedom to move and think, it's about getting sufficient emotional balance to see the situation more clearly and make better decisions.

The process is not necessarily about leaving someone else. This is not about desertion or divorce. Rather, this process is directed at helping you either to find your self, perhaps for the first time, or to get back the self you had but seem to have abandoned as you developed an unhealthy attachment.

Some of us have never really quite had a self, though on the outside we may have looked just fine. For the majority of our lives our decisions, behaviors, and language have been based more on what others might think of us, or want us to do or be. We have had an extremely external focus that observes our environment, then dictates what we should say or do, and we have faithfully followed that external lead. We have in some ways been rewarded for this external focus—pleasing others, minimizing conflicts, often being the ones to see that responsibilities get taken care of. We are seen as reliable and responsible. It has become an identity of ours, and nothing is wrong with this identity in and of itself. The problems arise when this identity is based almost entirely on external demands and expectations. The internal self has been neglected and is not known or can scarcely be heard. The process of disentangling invites and fosters a focus on the internal self: What do *I* need, want, feel, believe, and think?

Others of us have cultivated a more balanced identity over the years, have been aware of our self and able to assert that self adequately. And then, without our awareness, we began to lose that self in our relationship with another person. Twelve-step literature describes the disease of addiction as "cunning, baffling, and powerful." Well, our vulnerability to unhealthy attachments can also be cunning, baffling, and powerful. Without our realizing it, we can allow our self to be eroded for what we believe is the benefit of the relationship to which we are attached.

The "Ideas for Disentangling" are intended to help *you* get in touch with *you*. The process does not predict what will happen to your relationship as a result of your disentangling. Disentangling is not the unhealthy game of backing off so the other person will come closer; it is not about scaring the other person into doing something you want them to do. It is not intended for the manipulation of others in any way. Disentangling is something you do for you, to help you get your feet back on the ground, to help you become less confused and have more serenity in your life.

Your relationship may benefit from your disentangling, in that it probably will interrupt the unhealthy patterns that have developed. As you change and act differently in the relationship, it is only natural that others in the relationship will also change. Through your changes, you are changing the dynamics of the relationship system.

We have no idea, however, how the other person may change in response. Change is hard for all of us. It is fair to expect that initially your change will not be well received, and the other person may try in a variety of ways to get things back to how they used to be, even if things were unhealthy. We, too, may retreat to the old patterns—we are attracted to the familiar. When things were not so good, we each at least knew how to act and react. Now, as things change, neither of us is as clear about what to say or do next.

Your disentangling does not guarantee your relationship will improve or be ideal; it likewise does not guarantee that your relationship will end. Your disentangling does offer you the opportunity to find you and, thereby, have some solid ground under your feet when you feel buffeted by the winds of the relationship. It offers you the opportunity to get off the roller coaster you've been on, and to just watch it for a while, so that you can then decide what you want to do.

THE BASICS
It's about Getting Balance

Many of us who are prone to entanglements are also prone to extremes. We believe we have to give *all* of our self *or none* of our self. We have to have *all* of their attention, or we want nothing to do with them. We think we have to meet every request or need of theirs, or they will be gone—we usually opt for giving all of our self to the other. So, when I suggest to a person that we focus on their needs rather than the needs of another, it is not unusual for them to ask me, "Wouldn't that be selfish?" They have immediately jumped in their thinking from the extreme of losing their self in another person to the extreme of complete selfishness. There *is* a middle ground.

We need to learn to live in the gray. We tend to see things as black or white, all or nothing. Living in the gray is a real challenge for those of us driven by our insecurities, who demand to know what's going on right now and what it all means. In the absence of solid information, our own fears and worries fill in the blanks. Then we jump to extremes: "It's over." "He doesn't love me at all." "She never loved me." "I'll never be happy and loved in a relationship." "I'm not lovable at all." "I never was lovable anyway."

Finding a balance in our thoughts, feelings, and behaviors is an indispensable part of disentangling. It may not be unhealthy for you to be in a particular relationship, if you can strike a balance between your focus on the other and your focus on your self. We don't necessarily have to end a relationship if we can find a point where our own needs are equally considered and respected.

One way to work on this balance is to think of things not necessarily as *either/or*, but rather as *both*.

A client was talking to me about an upcoming week-long holiday visit to her mother's home. Her mother was active in her addiction and lived alone. My client was very torn about how to handle this visit. She was feeling guilty because she had not visited in a long time and was worried about her mother's drinking. On the other hand, she was feeling very disinclined to go. She knew how hard it was to be around her emotionally dependent mother, whose depression, fears, and anger could be overwhelming. Should she go or not?

"Perhaps there is something in the middle," I suggested. "You don't have to go for the entire week, nor do you have to not go at all. Perhaps you could do some of both."

"I never thought of that," she said.

That's right. We don't think of *both*. We think of either/or. We think things have to be either this way or that way. We think we have to give completely of our self or not at all.

In another variation on this theme, someone called me on the telephone to wish me happy birthday. It was a brief call of about five minutes, during which the caller and I talked mostly about her. When I got off the phone, my husband commented that it was really something that she'd called to wish me happy birthday and then spent the whole time talking about her. I quickly pointed out that it was a factor of *both* me and her. Though this person does often talk about her self, I was aware I encouraged that as a way of not talking about my self. It was neither her fault nor mine; it was *both*.

Another example of this was taught to me by a favorite grad school professor. I received clinical supervision from her while working on my courses for licensure. She suggested that I replace the word "but" with the word "and." For example, "I love my husband, *but*

I am mad at him." The construction of this sentence implies that these are separate concepts, and the use of the word "but" almost suggests that being angry with my husband cancels out loving him or that both can't exist simultaneously. If we instead say, "I love my husband, *and* I am mad at him," we acknowledge that *both* things are true and present. And both things can exist at the same time. It doesn't have to be one or the other. We need to own both. It is what will help us get well.

Living with *both* is living in the gray, in the middle—not choosing one thing or another or having to be all or nothing. Disentangling is about finding the balance for your self. This is a moment-by-moment process that requires you to be aware of your extremes, to creatively determine what may be a healthier middle ground for you.

The concept of a continuum can be useful. Rather than the broad label of "codependent," I prefer to address codependence as codependent behaviors. By looking at codependent behaviors, we are better able to define the things we are doing that create tangles and loss of self. These specific behaviors—behaviors such as helping, fixing, caretaking, people-pleasing, and conflict-avoiding—can be examined on a continuum, from okay to going too far. Our all-or-nothing thinking may have convinced us that in order to recover we need to stop these behaviors completely. Most are natural, desirable human behaviors and do not need to be discontinued. Our recovery hinges on our learning to notice these behaviors, understanding that they are okay within a certain range on the continuum, and developing skills to help us not carry them too far. This dynamic balance is crucial to learning to disentangle.

A Continuum for Understanding and Managing Codependent Behaviors

Any particular **codependent behavior** can be examined along this continuum:

OKAY ★————————————————|————————————✗ **TOO FAR**

Keeps connection with self	Loses connection with self
Is able to be flexible and open	Is rigid or obsessed
Causes no impairment in functioning	Causes impairment in functioning
Has a secure attachment with self	Has an insecure attachment with self

---

This continuum illustrates how we might distinguish okay behaviors from behaviors that go too far. We are in the "okay" zone as long as we stay aware of our self and our behaviors, are not obsessed and compulsive in our thoughts and actions, are not causing our self problems, and are not driven by our fears and insecurities. We can trust our self and remain centered.

Going too far is where this loss of self can become addictive. At this end of the continuum, the balance of self and other is way off. We are not listening to our self, not considering our self, not acting on our own behalf. Our fears and insecurities are quite active and control many of our choices. Obsessive thoughts and compulsive behaviors are present and difficult to manage. We are causing problems for our self and interfering with the growth and capabilities of the other person.

Our job is to learn how to live in the healthy range of this continuum, with awareness and care for self, as we offer our self to others. To notice when we are slipping into our preoccupations and desires for the other person and to adjust our self back into health. To let go of the all-or-nothing approach and be able to discern when more or less is appropriate in a specific situation.

As you start on this work, you may find at first that you move from one extreme to the other. For example, you may go from trying to help someone every day to not helping them at all. You may skip the middle. This is not unusual in early recovery. We have such little experience living in the gray that we are apt to miss the mark when we first start trying. Once I have jumped from one extreme to the other and become aware of it, then my task is gradually to move my self from this other extreme toward the middle, as much as I am able. Instead of not helping this other person at all, I can learn to ask them if I can help them and in what ways. I then decide which of their suggestions I can really do and still be in the "okay" range of the continuum.

This is living in the gray.

THE BASICS
It's about Intervening on Your Own Behalf

In the field of addiction treatment, we do interventions on the addict. A group of caring and knowing family and friends get together with the addict, usually with professional help, and confront them about their disease. With love and concern, they describe the specific behaviors of the addict they are worried about, and the problems they have caused. In other words, they *intervene.* The primary goal of the intervention is to get the addict to go into treatment for their disease in order to recover.

Intervening on your own behalf is about becoming aware of your own destructive patterns of thoughts, feelings, and actions, and making efforts to change these patterns for the better.

At first, intervening on your self is somewhat hard. The fact that you're reading this book, though, suggests some awareness that you may be ready for a change. When a client first comes to therapy, they are intervening on their own behalf. Even these first steps of seeking help are self-interventions.

As you progress in separating your self emotionally from the other person, you will hopefully gain a clearer picture of who you are and who they are. You will become more aware of who and what entangles you, what causes you to be entangled, and how you feel and act when you are entangled. With this awareness, as well as the skills you are developing, you can start to make more informed decisions about whether you want to act/react in the same old ways or instead do something different.

The goal is to become aware of the moment when you have this choice, this opportunity, to think, feel, and act differently. We encounter many of these moments over the course of a day. At any one of these specific moments, when we realize we are feeling that familiar way, talking in that usual way, about to act/react in that predictable way, *this* is when we can say to our self, "Oh, I know what's going on here, and I don't want to keep doing this!" *This* is the moment we can tell our self to stop and to go a different route. Twelve-step programs define insanity as continuing to do the same thing and expecting different results. Let's do something different on our own behalf. Let's intervene on our insanity.

When I am pursuing an argument too far, I am aware that I keep bringing up the same issues, keep asking the other person the same questions, and keep following them from room to room. When I start this following-around stuff, I know that's the moment for me to *intervene on my own behalf*. That's the moment for me to stop my self—to take a walk, call a friend, do whatever I need to do to help me take a break from this argument and get some healthy distance from it, so I can think more clearly and have more serenity. Pursuing this argument will not give me clarity and serenity. I have to remind my self of this.

I have to be the one to make this change for my self. I am the one who has to have sufficient awareness of my own thoughts, feelings, and behaviors to see the opportunity to do something different. I am the one who has to be developing my own boundaries so that I can actually *do* something different for my self in that moment.

It's about Spiritual Growth

Through my participation in a twelve-step fellowship I have heard that "religion is for people who are afraid of going to hell, and spirituality is for people who have been there."

The process of disentangling undoubtedly calls for spiritual growth. Our entanglements have often evolved from the belief that we alone can control and create what we want in our relationship with the other person. Though we may not necessarily be aware of it, our thoughts and actions have reflected our belief that if we say or do things in just the right way at just the right time with just the right expression and tone, then we can get what we want from this entangled relationship. We act as though we are in control. We "force solutions." We think we know exactly what is best and how things should happen. We act like we're the ultimate power. Either we are in charge, or we think the person with whom we are entangled is a "god" and therefore has the power. And our lives go to hell.

Spirituality is about coming to the belief that there is a power greater than our self and allowing that higher power to be a living presence in our lives.

The process of disentangling is about *both* intervening on your own behalf *and* letting go and letting your higher power act on your behalf.

The key concept here is the development of some belief in a power greater than your self. You decide who or what that power is for you. Your higher power may be the God you know through your religious faith. Your higher power may be a personal God you have come to know on your own. You may yet be discovering your higher power.

Spiritual growth is about cultivating this belief in a higher power. It can be a wonderful, freeing experience to realize you are ultimately *not* the one in charge and to learn to let go of things you cannot control to this higher power.

Learning what you can and cannot control is an essential part of this process of disentangling. We start by thinking we can control most everything, or at least we give it a good try. Then, as we hit our head against the wall, if we are lucky we begin to see that just maybe we can't make happen what we want to have happen. We can offer the situation what is reasonable, and then we have to let go and let God.

We've all heard it before: You can lead a horse to water, but you can't make it drink. We can make an offering, a gift so to speak, to the other person, and then we have to simply stand by and let them do with it as they will. We are not their higher power. They have their own.

In order to let go of things beyond our control, it is important to develop faith—faith that we are not alone, that a power greater than our self is in fact present and attentive. So when we let go, we are not falling into the abyss of emptiness and darkness, rather we are relaxing into the arms of a power that is there for us and will provide for us what we *really* need.

I am reminded of a couple of things we say in my twelve-step program:

"What I need to know will come to my attention without any effort on my part."

"What I need will be there for me."

And a short prayer I made up one lonely, unhappy Christmas Eve in the second year of my recovery:

"God,

If it's me, help me to know.

If it's not, help me to let go."

As I said this prayer that Christmas Eve, outside in the dark of my driveway, I felt comfort and relief. I was not alone. I was not in charge. I was not totally responsible for all the ills of my life or their cures. My higher power was there, too, ready and available to share these self-imposed burdens, to support me and protect me. All that was required of me was to reach out for this spiritual help.

This can, however, truly be a challenge sometimes. Even as we cultivate our belief in a power greater than our self, it is easy to get caught up in a situation and slip into our super-controlling behaviors. We may not be aware that once again we are trying to manipulate, manage, or control someone, that we are once again acting like we know what is best for all of us.

Spiritual growth requires not only the belief in a power greater than your self, but also the practice of making contact with that higher power. Daily practice. Moment-to-moment contact, if desired. Prayer, meditation, monologues, dialogues, writing, walks, contact with nature, with children, time alone—whatever it is that helps you get in touch with your higher power is what I mean by practice.

We can be so busy with our daily lives that it becomes easy to slip into our rip-and-run mode, and by extension, employ our push-and-pull techniques on the people and events in our life. By regularly making our self available to contact with our higher power, we can consciously sort through what we can and cannot control, and release our self with comfort and serenity from those things beyond our control.

THE BASICS
It's a Process without Rules or Sequence

We know this book is designed around the original handout "Ideas for Disentangling." Please note the first word: "Ideas." That's just what they are. Ideas. Yes, carefully thought-through ideas, born of experience and tested through yet more experience. But they are offered here only as ideas.

This process of disentangling does not require you to do such and such. There is no clear and proper formula for achieving the emotional and personal clarity we work toward. There is no recipe for success here.

Clients often ask, "What is the *right* thing to say?" "What is the *right* thing to do?" "Do you think I did *the right thing*?"

Well, I don't know.

A more helpful question to ask our self might be "Did I listen to me and respond in a way true to what I heard from me?" "Did I speak or act in a way that respected my own needs as well as the other person's?"

Those of us who get entangled are often people who want to do things the right way. We want very much to please others, and we certainly don't want to create any conflict. Avoiding conflict is the overriding concern, and many of our decisions about what to say and do may be based on this drive to keep things running smoothly.

So it is no surprise that questions come up for us, like "Should I . . .?" "Was it okay that I. . .?" "Was it wrong for me to . . .?"

The process of disentangling, however, has no rules. There are no "shoulds" or "should nots." The process of disentangling is about finding the answers for your self. It's about creating emotional space for you, so you can listen to your needs, feelings, and thoughts. Granted, this may be listening to you for the first time in your life, or you may have limited experience in listening to you. So, at first you may not be hearing much, or you may not be aware of what you are hearing. And this may press you to ask, "Now what should I do?"

Disentangling involves your continuing to listen to you—talking to knowledgeable others, doing some writing, having some quiet time—so you can figure out what *you* need to say or do. It's a process that invites us to move from being focused on the external to focusing on the internal, away from external expectations and directions toward the internal feelings and thoughts that truly provide much of the information we seek.

A client came to see me with these issues. He entered therapy because he'd been having a very hard time letting go of a romantic relationship. For the past three years he'd been seeing a woman he'd met through a colleague at his law firm. The first two years of their relationship had been enjoyable and mutual. Over the past year, however, his partner had distanced herself from him in noticeable ways. By the time he started to work with me, they were no longer together and were barely talking. My client didn't understand this change in their relationship and was very reluctant to accept it. In one particular therapy session, he wondered whether or not to send his former partner a card congratulating her on the promotion she'd received at work.

There is no right or wrong answer for this client in this case. He will have to figure out what's best for him. We talked about his question in this way. We looked at his motivations for wanting to send the card. We looked at possible expectations he may have if he sends the card. We looked at what his message to his former partner would be. In the end, he said he wouldn't send the card if it upsets *him* too much. He left the session with plans to keep listening to his self to decide this.

We are again living in the gray. In the absence of rules and prescriptions, we have to figure out many of these answers for our self. And while we do, we are in the gray. There are not necessarily many yes-or-no answers. It is often not appropriate or helpful to simply say, "Do this" or "Don't do that." We have to live a while with wondering and not knowing. And while we do, we just keeping focusing on our self and making contact with our higher power.

Likewise, there is no proper sequence of steps for disentangling. Yes, my outline of ideas was written in a specific order, mostly for clarity and logic. It is necessary to Face Our Illusions before we can work on Detachment and Boundaries. Our Illusions can keep taking us back into our hopes and dreams, further away from realities. Our spiritual growth plays an equal role in this process. Some people have suggested that Spirituality should be listed first on the outline, and I understand their reasoning.

The point is that disentangling means working with ideas from any of the four sections at any point in time, which is to say, working with all four sections at the same time. This isn't a checklist. What you think you have completed today may be your assignment again tomorrow. These issues keep coming up, and we keep returning to these "Ideas for Disentangling" and applying them, situation by situation. To this end, as I've mentioned, I prefer to think of the four areas of disentangling as a circle rather than a list.

Hopefully, as you go through this process of disentangling, you'll feel less lost and more quickly able to find you, your higher power, and your new skills and awareness. This will come to you as you work simultaneously with your Illusions, Detachment, Boundaries, and Spirituality. They all interrelate. They are all important. Our growth comes from working in these areas in no particular order other than the order we find best meets our needs in a particular situation, at a particular moment.

THE BASICS
It's a Process That Takes Time

Recently I was in America's "largest gift shop" on an East Coast beach. On the shelf were attractive sand sculptures. One of them was a wizard in a flowing royal purple robe, holding a glowing emerald green crystal ball. I was charmed, and thought of putting it in my office as a friendly, ironic comment on the process of changing our self.

We'd like to think we can change our self in an instant. We want, and sometimes even need, a quick cure.

Just the week before, I had felt the need to qualify to a new client the limits of my services. She seemed to have had some impression of my being able to do great things to transform her life. I had to explain to her that I was not in any form a wizard working magic.

Rather, I see my self as joining with her on a journey to work on the things that have brought her to counseling. I believe that many of the answers she seeks are already within her, and we can work toward her hearing those answers and responding to them.

My experience is that this journey takes a while. In fact, I do not think of it as ending. It simply becomes the path we take as we live our lives.

Yes, I believe we can fairly quickly start to see things differently and learn new skills to help us make some changes. It's the *application* of this new learning that can be slow in coming.

We may start seeing our illusions and attend more to the reality of our situation. That reality may suggest that it is not in our best interest to continue a particular relationship. Behaviorally, however, we may be a long way from the ability to act on this new understanding. We may well continue in the relationship until we have more clarity, greater detachment, better boundaries, and stronger spirituality. That is what we need to do. And that is okay.

We need to be patient with our self. We need to stay on our path of healing as best we can, kindly reassuring our self that we are doing the best we can as fast as we can. As the twelve-step programs so consistently remind us, we were not made this way in a day, so we cannot expect to become different in a day.

Many of us have had our entangling thoughts and behaviors for years. They have been the very way we see and respond to the world. If we are a people-pleaser, we have sought to please most everyone we've come in contact with, from parents, to teachers, to bosses, to our dentist. If we tend to avoid conflict, and in so doing ignore our own needs, we do this in most settings and with most people. These styles of thinking, feeling, and behaving are ingrained, which is why it has been so hard for many of us to see them in the first place.

The creation of more balance and serenity in our lives requires a major overhaul of our systems. Twelve-step thinking is different from what most of us are used to. It does imply a "brain washing" of sorts—a most refreshing washing, actually. And this brain washing takes time.

Disentangling is a process of deep changes. It is about learning to become aware of our self, when for years our focus has been outside our self. It is about seeing our self as separate from and relating to others, when for years we have been entangled. It is about setting boundaries, when for years we have had none. It is about living with and turning over to our higher power things that we have no control over, when for years we've been trying to do it all on our own.

These changes cannot be had quickly. There is no wizard. There is no wizard on my office shelf, either. I decided against it, though he truly was lovely and inviting, as is the desire for a quick, miraculous cure.

The main thing is that these changes *can* be had. We can transform our lives. We can make these deep changes. We just need to be patient and realistic with our self as we travel on this journey, noticing the smaller successes along the way. They will be there, though they may not be the larger successes you think you want. Make sure to honor them as they occur; they are stepping stones in your journey. If you don't see them and honor them, you may lose your way. If you do see and honor them, they will help you with the next step.

Disentangling is a process that takes time. It may take longer than you wish, but it is worth every bit of time invested. We are transforming our lives. Hopefully, as the changes come, piece by piece, we will reach the point where we can never go back to how we used to be. And making such changes really does take a while.

THE BASICS
Every Day Ain't Great

We all make mistakes. We know what we want to do for our self in a situation and find that we "blow it." We successfully set a limit with someone one day, only to find that we can't set a similar limit with someone else the next day. We have days that feel just like the old days—agitated, preoccupied, and anxious. We think poorly of our self, and tell our self we've learned nothing.

Part of why it can take a good while to make changes in our lives is the reality that we won't do everything perfectly the first time.

This is a warning. Every day and every interaction won't show your progress. This is normal. Be not discouraged. The twelve-step programs tell us, "Two steps forward, one step back."

To expect *every* day to be great is unrealistic, symptomatic of our black-and-white thinking, our gravitation toward all or nothing. Facing this reality can be sad. We'd really like for things to go well all the time.

Back in the early 1980s, my husband and I were visiting his family's home on a lake in Maine. One day we rented an aluminum boat with a small motor, and gently cruised from Naples, at our end of the lake, to Harrison at the other end. The day was gorgeous, with blue skies and warm sun. We were in no hurry, and dawdled along as we wished, checking out islands and bays, houses and wildlife. We enjoyed each other's company, comfortably sharing chat and silence. It was a great day. I have often wished that every day could be like that, and in a friendly, fun way, I have adopted the reminder that "Every day ain't a boat trip to Harrison."

No, every day isn't a sunny, relaxed trip in a boat. In fact, some days I'm more apt to say, "I am not going down with this ship!" Of course there are days when I feel very insecure, very anxious, very discouraged, believing that at any moment I may lose the things that are significant to me. Sometimes reality suggests that bad things may indeed happen, that the ship actually may sink. These are not great days, in fact they can be downright difficult. The goal is not to drown. Let the ship go down, but don't be on it.

What's needed is to start to see the path you are on as you move from entanglements to centeredness and serenity. The path is not a straight line. It has curves, detours, and obstacles. These curves are like switchbacks up a mountain—you travel a long way, only to find you haven't gained much altitude. You come around a bend only to find something in your path. Your journey is slowed.

Some boat trips start out warm and sunny. The sky is blue, the water calm, the mood relaxed. And then, seemingly out of nowhere, a dark and ominous thunderstorm appears, bringing turbulence and unrest.

Our path is the constant through all of this. Our path consists of things we are learning: about our self, about our entanglements, and about ways to help our self detach, set boundaries, and develop our spirituality. Our path is a focus on our self and our relationship with our higher power.

Your path will be your own. No one's is exactly the same. Our paths reflect our uniqueness. Your path will be cultivated by you. Certainly, this book offers some ideas on the general construction of your path, but it is yours to create.

Some stretches of your path will be clearer than others. Sometimes you may have to stop for a while to determine the next direction to take. The good news, though, is that you will not feel lost again, the way you did when you were entangled.

My experience is that every day ain't great. I make mistakes, and I have setbacks. My experience is also that even when this happens,

I am able to find my self again much more quickly than in the past. And I do not feel lost. I understand what I have done, and I understand what I can do to retrieve my peace and clarity.

THE BASICS
Don't Go It Alone

Entanglements invite us to isolate. We become so focused on the other person that we drop everything else. We decline opportunities with friends; we skip out on previous commitments; we even neglect our responsibilities to work, to our family, and to our self. At a certain point, nothing seems more important than whatever is going on with the other person.

We become isolated. And that isolation adds to our craziness.

Without input from sources outside the problem, our thinking can get even more obsessive and irrational. We can't seem to think of much, other than that with which we are entangled. And often our contacts with that person only add to our craziness, rather than untangle it. They say things to us and about us that we either totally accept or totally discount. After a conversation with the person with whom we are entangled, we may end up feeling we are the problem completely. We feel worse, more confused than when we began.

We want to believe we can talk to the person and resolve the things we want to resolve, so we repeatedly go to them to talk once more about all of this. And once more we find our self tangled and stuck.

It never even occurs to us to go talk to someone else.

Talking with someone else can help us to free our self from this tangled web. Talking with someone else does not mean having them tell you what to do; it means discussing your issues, listening to what is said to you, and then doing with the discussion whatever you may.

Talking with someone else helps to break up our thoughts and thus create new and different thoughts and possibilities. We get new ideas and can see things in a new light, more objectively and more realistically. No doubt our perceptions have become distorted. We have constantly adjusted to unacceptable situations and behaviors, and in this adjusting our perceptions have been altered. An outside reality check can be most useful in helping to correct our perceptions.

Talking with someone else can also help us not feel so alone. As our isolation has increased, so has our loneliness. In part this is ironic. We think we are pursuing this entangled relationship because we want to be in a relationship and have companionship. The reality, however, is often that we are very lonely in the entangled relationship. It provides little to no good, healthy companionship. It is a very lonely relationship.

We may also feel lonely because we tell our self all sorts of unhealthy things. We tell our self that:

- No one would understand my problem or situation.
- No one else has this problem.
- This is stupid that I have this problem.
- I am too embarrassed to tell anyone about this situation.
- I can handle this on my own.
- It's too late to do anything about this problem now.
- I'm not supposed to talk to anyone outside my family about my troubles.
- Other people may be nice and listen, but they really don't care.

- I tried this before but it didn't help.

- No one can help me.

Between our entangled relationship and our own trapping thoughts, we have become stuck. Reaching out to others can help to change this.

Remember to be selective as you choose people with whom to talk. Toby Rice Drews addresses this well in *Getting Them Sober*. She speaks of the need for us to talk to people who understand the difficulties of entanglements, addictions, and relationships. If we talk to people who don't understand our experiences, we are likely to get unhelpful advice, biased points of view, or even plain old gossip. None of this helps us to disentangle; in fact, it can often complicate things more. We become even more confused and angry, sad, and hopeless.

Our family members or best friends, though they may be deeply concerned and want good things for us, often simply don't know what to say to help us. Their suggestions of "hang in there" or "give it another try," though well-intended, may not be in your best interest if you really tune in to them. Messages like "you don't want to upset so-and-so by doing something like that" suggest that we consider the needs of someone else more than our own. Disentangling suggests we consider our own needs just as seriously, if not more so, as we work out these difficulties.

So where are these people "in the know"? They can certainly be found in Al-Anon, the twelve-step fellowship for family and friends of addicts. This free support group is available in most communities in the United States and around the world. The Al-Anon welcome indicates that living with alcoholism can be too much for us as individuals. Similarly, living with an entanglement can be too much for most of us. We can't handle it alone. The experience, strength, and hope of the members of this fellowship can help us to recover. We are not told what to do in this group; rather, we gather information and inspiration, then use it in our lives as we wish and as we can.

Other people "in the know" can be found in the helping professions. They may be psychotherapists, addiction counselors, medical professionals, or ministers. Don't assume, however, that any of these people will understand your experiences simply because of their professional title. Shop around for the services you seek, keeping in mind that it is okay to inquire about a professional's credentials and areas of interest and expertise. Just because they are a psychologist does not mean they work well with addictions. They may not understand the experience of entanglement and the difficulties of extraction. Interview them. Let them know what you are looking for. Decide if they are the one to help you find and cultivate you.

Support groups can be another place to find healthy companionship. These groups may be offered by public and private mental health and addiction treatment programs and clinicians. Sometimes these groups are held in churches or are started by a grassroots group of individuals who share these issues. These groups may have in their name terms such as "relationship addictions," "healthy relationships," "codependency," or "loving too much." Whatever the title, I suggest you visit the group or participate in an intake session with a group leader to gather information to help you decide if they might be helpful to you.

Lastly, individuals can be of great support to us if they are patient and understanding about the complexity of our entanglements. They may be select friends or family members, an individual from a twelve-step program who we have asked to be our sponsor, or anyone else who happens into our life who we feel truly understands us and our situation.

Regardless of the messages you give to your self, you are not unusual or alone in what is happening to you. There are people out here who can join you in your efforts to disentangle. There is no need to go it alone. In fact, it is very difficult to disentangle successfully on your own.

Joining with others on this journey can be freeing and fun.

I invite you to join us.

6 THE FOUR AREAS OF WORK

"Each of the elements is very important to me, and I find them to be interwoven. This is not a step-one/step-two process. I use each of them, with awareness or not, situation by situation. When I look back at something that happened I can see, for example, how I detached, set some boundaries, and reminded my self of the reality of the situation."

This chapter offers a detailed look at practical ways to apply each of the specific "Ideas for Disentangling." I have divided it into the four sections described on the list: Facing Illusions, Detaching, Setting Healthy Boundaries, and Developing Spirituality.

The discussion of each idea has several sources: things I say as I explain the ideas to my self and to my clients, experiential activities we do in group and individual therapy sessions and the results that come from those activities, and the experiences of my clients as they work on releasing their self from their entanglements. All of this has been deeply influenced by the practicing of the words on the page by my self and many others.

I have attempted to offer the information in a brief, easily referenced form. Feel free to jump around as you read the ideas. Read the ideas that seem to apply to you most at the time. Read the ideas that attract your interest. Read the ideas that may confuse you or that you don't get. Read them in whatever order you desire.

Do read them all.

Remember, these are the nuts and bolts of helping our self to disentangle from someone else. They are the ingredients of transformation, from anxiety and obsession to serenity and centeredness.

Try on these ideas. See what works for you. And as you do, remember "The Basics" of the previous chapter: This is a process that focuses on you. This is a process about finding balance in your life. This is a process that involves you listening to you and your situation, and figuring out what works best for you. This is a process that involves belief in a power greater than your self.

Blending these "Ideas for Disentangling" with an understanding of how the process works, you can create a stronger and healthier you.

"You know, I think they have changed.
I don't think that will happen again."

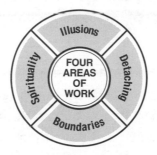

THE FOUR AREAS OF WORK

Facing Illusions

"Oh, what a tangled web we weave,
When first we practise to deceive!"

Sir Walter Scott (*Marmion* Canto VI, Stanza 17)

How true these famous lines ring, in terms of the entanglements I speak of.

In the case of our tangled webs, the deceiving we do is to our self. We create all sorts of illusions or false beliefs about the other person, about our self, and about our situation. Our illusions may also be called fantasies, dreams, or hopes.

Illusions are usually about what we think things are or what we want them to be, rather than the reality of what they are. And not only do we repeatedly create these illusions in our relationships, we also become very attached to them and are hard-pressed to let them go.

Facing Illusions can also be called Facing Reality. Not Facing Illusions can be called "denial," a word familiar in recovery treatment. Denial is minimizing what-is-so, acting like what-is-so did not happen, believing what-is-so will never happen again. Commonly identified as a factor that makes recovery from addictions difficult if not impossible, denial will do the same for our movement toward a healthy self.

I first started using the word "illusions" as a result of my work with a mentor. One day, as I was rattling on about changes I believed could happen in the behaviors of someone else, she stopped me and explained that illusions are the glue that holds all of the crazy-making together. She heard me holding on to beliefs that denied what-was-so. She heard me being ever-hopeful in the face of no more reasons to be hopeful. She helped me recognize that until I could see things for what they are, I would continue to be stuck in the problem. I saw the need to Face Illusions.

In order to disentangle our self, we must work with our denial. We must get in touch with the realities of us, them, and our situation. In order to free our self from the "stuckness" of our entanglements, we must find the truth and work to accept it. Doing so can help us begin to get some emotional balance and start seeing things in literally a new way.

FACING ILLUSIONS
Find the Truth about You, Them, and Your Situation

". . . and the truth shall make you free."

John 8:32.

The truth may set us free, *and* it may be hard to find.

Without our awareness, we live in our thoughts, our ideas, our hopes, our dreams. "Things will be so much better when," a client says to me.

We believe that though things may not be great today, they will be better tomorrow. "Though I'm starving today, one day I will sit at a great feast," explains another client.

We live with the hopes that others will change in the way we'd like them to. "I just know they'll treat me differently this time," says yet another client.

The disease of addiction is characterized by denial, denial that the specific manifestation of addiction is causing the individual and their family problems. Entanglements, too, are characterized by denial, denial that our unrealistic expectations, our inaccurate perceptions, and our fantasies about the other person are causing us problems.

As I have worked with Facing Illusions, both with myself and in workshops, the topic of hope regularly comes up. People ask if it is wrong to have hope that things will change. I suggest that it is okay, and even good, to be hopeful—up to a point. We want to believe that people and situations can change, that things will get better, that others will respond to conversations, limits, or treatment, but at some point we need to face the reality of the situation. Are things really getting better? Have things changed the way we need them to in order to stay with the relationship? At some point—which is very individual, arrived at through the self-discerning work you are learning to do here—we have to be with the reality of what is. This is not to suggest what to say or do beyond that point; it is only about Facing Illusions.

Facing Illusions requires us to see not only the reality of others and our situations with them, but the reality of our self as well. It

Disentangle: When You've Lost Your Self in Someone Else

requires us to be honest with our self about our motivations, our behaviors, our offers, and our demands, as well as our feelings, thoughts, and attitudes. Because we are so focused on the other person, it can be challenging to remember that we must look at the illusions we have about our self that keep us in the problem, that have us glued to the crazy-making.

Here are some specific examples of illusions that can feed our entanglements:

Illusions about Others and Our Relationship with Them

"They can't do this without me."

"If I don't do it, it won't get done at all."

"They need me to help in this way."

"They will leave me if I do this."

"They will leave me if I don't do this."

"They will fail if I don't help."

"If I say it enough times, they will get it."

"I can figure out how to get through to them."

Illusions about Self

"I am so caring and helpful."

"I only want what's best for them."

"I am not trying to control them."

"I will only say this one more time."

"I only did it for them."

"I am not angry."

"I don't expect anything in return."

"I can't live without them."

Our skill development in Facing Illusions involves identifying the specific illusions we may have, as illustrated by the statements above, then changing the language to make statements better anchored in honesty, accuracy, and reality. To attempt to Face Illusions and work toward the possibility of healthy changes for self, consider these alternatives to the above statements:

Realities about Others and
Our Relationship with Them

"They can do this without me."

*"If I don't do it, they may or may not do it,
and I can live with that."*

"I know they can do this on their own."

"I must do this for me even if they leave me."

*"I just can't do this,
even if they have to leave me."*

*"My help really isn't keeping them
from failing in the long run."*

*"My repeating my self will
not make things better."*

*"I have done all I can to help
them to understand."*

Realities about Self

*"I am so caring and helpful, and I am also
trying to have things my way."*

"I really don't know what is best for them."

"I am trying to control them."

"I am having trouble not repeating my self."

*"I did it to fix the situation and
ease my anxiety."*

"I am angry."

"I will be disappointed if they don't respond."

"I can live without them."

These alternative statements, which move us toward greater health, are difficult to construct. To do so requires that we see things from an entirely different perspective, a view from our inside out, with an honesty with our self that may feel entirely new. We haven't realized how we've been dishonest with our self and others, have actually probably felt quite honest, trustworthy, even noble. We have been the ones with our heads above water trying to save everyone else. Who would have thought?

Now we know. Now we know to watch for our illusions, to name them, and to find a more accurate statement about our self, the other person, and our situation with them. To do this, we do well to:

- See the person for who they are here and now.

- Pay attention to words *and* behaviors.

- Ask for clarity if we are confused or unclear.

- Stop making excuses, defending, and rationalizing.

- Live in the present and pay attention to all that is being said and done.

- Live in the present and pay attention to our feelings, thoughts, and behaviors.

- Remember that much of the truth we seek is right here now.

The truth is not necessarily bad; in fact, the truth may even be good news. It's just that often the truth is *different* than what we thought. As a client of mine frequently says, "I want to get into the reality."

Without the truth, we remain entangled. Our illusions can feed our hopes and dreams of controlling and changing things beyond our control. Our illusions take us into our fantasies and away from the reality of our lives.

Finding the truth is a necessary step in finding our self.

FACING ILLUSIONS
Illusions, Reality, and You

Think of a person or situation with
which you presently feel entangled.

What is a hope or belief you have
about this person or situation?

Look at the realities of you, them, and the situation:

What has happened that makes you believe
things will change for the better?

What has or has not happened that tells you
things may not change for the better?

Looking at this data, what is the present reality
about you, this person, and your situation?

Using the Illusion and Reality examples presented
in this section, write at least one illusion of yours
you are now aware of. State this illusion as simply
as you can. Don't judge it or try to correct it as you
write. Just let your beliefs come out.

Now, try to write an alternative statement based
on the realities of the data you discovered earlier
in this exercise. Again, don't judge your self, your
beliefs, or whether you are doing this correctly.
Let the statements come. See what illusions you
can move closer to reality.

FACING ILLUSIONS
Work to Accept the Truth You Find

"The Truth will set you free . . . but first it will piss you off!"

Bumper sticker on my friend's suitcase

Yes, once we've found the truth, it may make us mad. It may make us sad. We may have trouble really believing it.

Regardless of whether the truth we come to understand is good news or bad, it is *a change*. It involves letting go of beliefs and hopes and dreams, saying goodbye to what we thought things were or could be, even fundamentally changing our perceptions.

It's no wonder we resist facing our illusions—not only are they essential to our entanglements, they are emotionally difficult to release. We may resist in a variety of ways, including re-adopting illusions, blaming others, or blaming our self. Facing our illusions does not feel good at first.

Working to accept the truth can be like working through the process of grieving, as described by Elisabeth Kübler-Ross in *On Death and Dying*. That process consists of five fundamental components: denial, anger, bargaining, depression, and acceptance. We most often associate grief with death. But grief comes with any loss, and Facing Illusions can certainly provide its share of loss— loss of hopes, dreams, ideas, beliefs, even loss of relationships, opportunities, and future plans.

As you worked on the "Illusions, Reality, and You" exercise above, examining your illusions and realities, you may have run into some challenging feelings related to grief. Perhaps you had trouble naming your illusions. Perhaps you were unhappy with the reality you named. Perhaps you did not like the exercise at all and resisted the notion of seeing things a different way, were uncomfortable with the letting go it requires, or were afraid of potential losses that could change your whole life. Maybe you found the reality you named to be a big relief. Any and all of these are normal feelings associated with grief.

Though the five components of grief—denial, anger, bargaining, depression, and acceptance—are described as stages, I suggest we think of them as components that may not happen in the listed order, taking us conclusively to acceptance. Rather, we move through these components in random order, feeling one thing one moment, another moment feeling something else. We may believe we have reached acceptance and find we are again feeling some of the other feelings. Each person's path through grief is different, and each has its own time frame, which cannot be set or rushed.

Here are five skills you can use to work with your grief and find your way to accepting the realities of you, them, and your situation:

- **Recognize and name the feelings** that come up for you as you state the reality of things to your self. We tend to notice more what we are thinking than what we are feeling, but our feelings are right there all along if we just shift our focus to them. Name them. Put them on a little list: upset, disappointed, frustrated, disturbed, sad, glad, relieved, etc.

- **Remember these are not a bunch of unrelated feelings** making you believe you must be crazy as you move from one to the other or that there is a really long list of things wrong with you. These feelings are all related to grief. They are natural responses to having to let go of something and to the losses that come with any change. You are already working on changes as you face your illusions.

- **Allow these feelings.** Try not to avoid them by distracting your self, becoming busy, shifting your focus to possibly another illusion that may somewhat relieve the grief you are feeling now. Simply acknowledge and own whatever may be coming.

- **Stay with your discomfort so as not to retreat to the illusions** that no longer work for you. As we move through denial in our recovery, it is tempting to return to what we always did or always believed; it is what we are familiar with. In its own way it is our place of comfort even if we are excruciatingly uncomfortable. Beware the power of your illusions to call you back. They can.

- **Trust this process.** Trust your self. This is all new. Asking you to trust in this process and your self is a big assignment, since we are just starting to turn our focus to our self. It is often only over the long haul that accepting the truth feels good and freeing. As we begin this healing process, we do well to remember and trust that we can free our self from our entanglements by finding and accepting the truth about our self, the other person, and our situation as we are willing and able, over and over again.

FACING ILLUSIONS
Grief And You

**When you come across a quiet, focused period
of time, spend some of it with these five skills
for dealing with grief:**

Recognize and name your feelings.

Remember these feelings are all related to grief.

Allow your feelings.

Stay with any discomfort that may arise in you.

Trust this process of recognizing and allowing
in order to heal.

**Allow the words that describe each skill
to settle in, educating you about what's
happening with your feelings, and the
importance of the work you are doing.**

**Reread what you wrote about your illusions and
the realities you were able to recognize in the
"Illusions, Reality, and You" exercise.**

**Then settle into noticing, allowing, naming, and
sticking with the feelings that come up for you. These
feelings may be about the content of your illusions
and realities, as well as this process of challenging
your own beliefs and behaviors.**

**Make a few notes about what you feel, practicing
simple recognition and allowing these feelings
without judgment and without having to do anything
about them at this time.**

"I let her affect me . . . all-consuming."

"'What do you want on your pizza?' I was asked. I don't know. I couldn't think. I just used to go along with what they wanted rather than try to decide what goes on a pizza that I would like."

"If I had a favorite color, what would it be?"

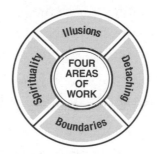

THE FOUR AREAS OF WORK
Detaching

"Everything that's happened wrong is my fault."

Detachment is a word I have come to know through my twelve-step program, which defines it as a recovery tool. Detachment means that I am not responsible for the addiction or recovery of the other person. I can let go of my attachments to trying to manage, fix, or control their addiction, and live my own life.

Detachment in this sense means not suffering because of others, not allowing my self to be used or abused by others, and not doing for others what they can do for their self. Detaching allows me to see things more realistically and make decisions that are ultimately better for me and the other person.

Indeed, I think of detachment as a way to back off from a situation, so I can bring it into focus and see it more clearly. Until I detach, I am right up in the face of the situation, perhaps literally up in the face of the individual with whom I'm entangled. This type of contact leaves me with blurred vision and a narrow, often distorted perception.

Detachment enables me to better see reality.

Detachment is not necessarily about leaving the other person physically, though sometimes this is the best thing to do, either at the moment or permanently. This section on detachment, however, is directed at helping you to get emotional balance for your self. Then you can see much better what's going on, and decide for your self about the issue of physical separation.

The ideas listed here are specific things we can do in our interactions with others to help us get this emotional balance They are the "how-tos" of detaching. It is only partially useful to say to a person that they should not allow their self to be used or abused, if they don't know how to make this happen. These ideas on detachment aim to help us know what to do in order to not suffer, to not be used or abused, and to not do for others what they can do for their self.

These ideas involve looking at our self and our vulnerability to entanglements. Understanding these things about our self and our history can help us to become less vulnerable.

They also involve changes in the ways we interact with others. When detaching, we slow down our interactions and work toward acting, rather than reacting to others.

All of the ideas relate to learning more about our self, listening to our self as we interact with others, and protecting both our serenity and our awareness that we have both feet firmly on the ground and cannot be knocked off balance.

Become Aware of Who and What Entangles You

- With whom do you get entangled?
- What entangles you with this other person?
- What parts of you get entangled?
- How do you act and feel when you're entangled?

Detaching is about getting emotional balance as you are dealing with a person or situation.

In order to detach, we must first become aware of with whom and what we may be entangled. The four questions above are all interrelated—they are all about this awareness-raising within us.

The more we understand what's in us that makes us vulnerable to entanglements, the more we can take care of our self. The more aware and knowing we become, the more we can intervene on our own behalf.

We can better understand our vulnerabilities to entanglement by examining who we are and what happened to us as we grew up. It is useful to look at how people treated us, and how we reacted to their treatment. What did we learn about our self then? What did we learn about others? How did we cope? Survive? Develop? All of these are sources of influence that leave us prone to entanglements.

As we look at these sources of our loss of self in others, I find it useful to organize them in the following way:

The diagram's core is the Individual. This is who we are genetically and biologically. It includes our basic tendencies of personality and relating. Yes, these are also affected by the next two concentric circles, but we probably have some basic tendencies before all of the external factors come into play.

The second layer, Family Systems, invites us to look at what we learned and how we responded to what happened to us as we grew up in our home.

And the third, Social/Cultural/Political Worlds, asks us to look beyond our family to our cultural experiences, to the teachings and values of the world in which we were raised. Where in the world were we raised? Where in the world did we hear or learn that?

These concentric circles bleed into each other. The elements I've placed in one circle (for the sake of teaching) may well be affected by elements in the neighboring circle. Our family was strongly affected by the social/cultural/political world in which they lived. Our basic tendencies of personality and relating were so affected by the behaviors of our parents, it can be hard to know what was first true about our being. Nevertheless, as a teacher I've arranged the information with this diagram in mind, placing pieces of education in a particular circle while knowing they are each colored by the neighboring circles. The educational pieces will be relatively brief, highlighting theories and evidence-based research related to these various influential sources. References will be cited, in case you wish to do further reading and self-study.

INDIVIDUAL INFLUENCES

The center circle represents our core self. Though it is hardly possible to define this core self without the outer-circle influences that start at birth (perhaps even in utero), we have some basic tendencies woven into who we are. These tendencies can be fostered and developed or thwarted as life proceeds. These tendencies may be genetic, or they may be learned very early on in our development. In either case, there are certain characteristics that may contribute to loss of self in others.

A readiness to extend self to others is one such characteristic, one which involves being kind, thoughtful, and considerate. It may manifest as generosity with time, resources, and heart. The very nature of the person is giving, with a sensitivity to others and the world around them. This person relates to the feelings and experiences of others and may easily be affected by their moods, attitudes, and needs. This core characteristic can extend to a desire to help and caretake, as well as to please others by reducing their pain and satisfying their needs.

Another characteristic is the ability to get things done. At the heart of this individual is the desire to be a hard worker and to do the work well. Related features include being focused and, once again, having the ability to take in the world around them and see what is needed or what might help. Reliability, loyalty, and dedication may well be additional tendencies that characterize this individual's core self.

A tendency toward anxiety may be present within an individual. Sometimes anxiety is situational, and sometimes it also has a biochemical basis, perhaps existing since early in life. An anxious nature may be expressed in several different ways. Worry and trouble controlling worry can be hallmarks of anxiety. Additionally, anxious symptoms can include body tension, difficulty concentrating, restless or unsatisfying sleep, being easily fatigued, and irritability.

Anxiety can mean unnecessary worry about a number of things. It tends to be an almost ever-present internal feature through which the individual's life is experienced. It can range from the gnawing uncertainty about whether the stove burners are turned off at home, to the catastrophic conclusion that not only are the burners on but the house is on fire and all the pets will die. These distressing thoughts disturb both the psyche and the body and can move the individual toward action on their worry and away from life as they were leading it in that moment. For those inclined to it, worry is powerful and tenacious.

Anxiety can also present itself through obsessive thinking. Obsessive thinking is another form in which thoughts are disturbed by anxious underpinnings. The mind keeps going over and over the same thing. It is stuck in a track of thought, highly resistant to moving off and moving on.

Compulsive behaviors are yet another way anxiety can express itself. The individual may have a tendency toward order, rules, or lists. They may have a strong need to have things a particular way and be unable to let go of this need until it is satisfied. Much like obsessive thinking, compulsive behavior moves in and is difficult to let go of.

Compulsive behaviors can become our addictions; addictions operate in this same way. The person loses the ability to control their use of a substance or a behavior or a relationship. Examples of addiction include alcohol, other drugs, gambling, sex, pornography, spending, shopping, eating, and relationships. With some substance addictions, the substance itself is addictive, which adds to this loss of control. But many of these addictions are fed by a tendency within the individual to find something in their sphere of life that attracts them, which gives them pleasure and relieves their basic anxiety and then becomes the dominant focus of their thoughts and actions.

Both clinically and practically speaking, what is behind these obsessive thoughts and compulsive behaviors is the desire to control anxiety. This may be conscious or not, and may contribute to a broader tendency to be controlling. Our control of people, places, and things can help us to feel calmer, to have things in the order we think they should be, and to simply feel like we are in charge of our lives, as opposed to having things happen helter-skelter around us and to us.

DETACHING

Entanglements and You

INDIVIDUAL INFLUENCES

Take a moment to study the concentric circle diagram illustrating Individual, Family, and Social/Cultural/Political influences. Without considering details, just take in the notion of your self as that core individual, with these various factors and experiences that affect who and how you are.

Now focus on the center circle, the Individual, and let that be you. As you do this work, remember that this is about learning about your self. It is not about judging, criticizing, or blaming your self. It is simply about increasing awareness of your characteristics so they can be your strengths and not become part of your problems.

Thinking about the ideas in this section on individual influences, do you identify with any of the specific tendencies that may contribute to entanglements:

Do you readily extend your self to others? Are you kind, thoughtful, and generous? Do you like to give of your self and your time to others?

Are you a hard worker who likes to get things done? Are you reliable and loyal?

Are you inclined toward anxiety?

Is worry familiar to you? Do you spend too much time with worry? Can it be hard to quiet your worry?

Can your thoughts become obsessive?

Do you have any behaviors that feel compulsive to you?

Do you have a tendency to be controlling?

Sit with what you are becoming aware of about you. Just sit with it. Knowing your self in a more complete, honest way is essential to the change you seek.

FAMILY INFLUENCES

The individual with these core tendencies can hardly be understood without a close look at the family system they grew up in. This is illustrated in the diagram by the concentric circle surrounding the center circle. The interplay of nature and nurture are at work here, and which one comes first remains unclear. We will continue simply to look at each of these pieces, and let each individual working toward their healthy self put the pieces in a place that helps them move forward with better understanding.

Taking time to look at what happened to us growing up can be powerful. Each of us likely has our own ways of protecting our self from certain facts and feelings about these early experiences. That's okay. This protection has actually been important to our survival. Now, as you open your self to looking more closely and honestly, some strong feelings may arise. When this happens, I suggest that you allow them, at the same time approaching them with a no-blame view as much as possible. People can be resistant to looking at their family systems because they don't want to blame or speak badly of family members. The idea here is to simply look at what happened to us growing up, what behaviors may have been modeled for us then, and to see how those experiences may be affecting us now. Doing this can ultimately free us. It can give us revelations, insights, and ideas about things we can do to release our true self.

Take care of you as you look at these origins. Work at your own pace, honoring your comfort and safety both physical and emotional. Look only as closely as you want to look. You may wish to immediately apply the information to your personal experiences, or you may read this academically as an assignment to learn about but not apply. Take breaks from what you are learning. Share your feelings and thoughts with people you can trust to understand and support your efforts.

The various sources of childhood and family influences on our loss of self in others can be organized under the following themes:

- True Self vs. False Self
- Secure vs. Insecure Attachment Styles
- Individuation vs. Fusion and Homeostasis
- Family Rules and Roles
- Trauma

Each of these areas of influence has been written about extensively. Each is fascinating to study, to apply the lens of codependency and see how our behaviors may have originated from some of these experiences and dynamics. What follows is an earnest attempt to inform you about these possible contributors to the loss of self in others, the central dynamic in codependency. The descriptions of these five areas are relatively brief, considering the volume of research that has been done. If your curiosity is piqued or you find that you identify strongly with what you are reading and wish to learn more, sources for further reading and study are provided.

True Self vs. False Self

In *The Drama of the Gifted Child: The Search for the True Self*, psychoanalyst Alice Miller helps us understand how in early childhood, part(s) of our true self may have been split off from us. Writing from her personal childhood experiences, Miller provides an informed and sympathetic look at the neglected, abused, or even battered child who is intelligent, alert, attentive, sensitive, transparent, reliable, and easy to manipulate. Miller explains several dynamics contributing to the development of a false self in response to such childhood experiences.

Beginning in infancy, the primary parent (whom Miller calls the mother but acknowledges can be another person) is not able to attune to the feelings and needs of the infant child. The parent is not able to mirror or echo what the infant is conveying to them. They are not empathetic, nor are they able to convey understanding to the child. The primary parent instead needs the child to satisfy the parent's needs and be the child the parent wants them to be. For the most part, these parental behaviors are not intentional. The primary parent's need to be mirrored and responded to by the child is often unconscious, likely the result of having received similar parenting themselves.

The infant child is perceptive and responsive to the needs and feelings of the primary caregiver. The child learns early to attune to the well-being of the parent. The child senses what their primary caregiver needs from them and responds accordingly with the feelings, behaviors, admiration, appreciation, and/or respect they know the parent wants from them. In so doing, the child disconnects from their own true feelings and true self.

The child learns that by fulfilling this role unconsciously assigned to them, they can meet the needs of the primary parent and garner a sense of security and love. Over time, the child continues to develop a strong capacity to attune to the feelings and needs of others and respond to those feelings and needs. They can carry this role into their relationships with siblings, with a partner and children, with anyone who conveys neediness. The child believes this is the way to receive love and be secure in a relationship. They believe this is the way to survive.

As a result of this pattern of attunement to others, the child's development of a healthy self is seriously compromised. Miller delineates three specific consequences to the individual as a result of this adaptation to the caretaker's needs.

The first is a loss of the ability to consciously experience particular feelings they may have. Certain feelings—perhaps joy, gratitude, satisfaction—may be allowed, whereas other feelings—such as anger, dislike, displeasure, or anxiety—may not be acceptable to the primary caregiver. As a result of this emotional editing, the child may push these feelings down, even stop noticing or recognizing them. These feelings have no place. In fact, the recognition and expression of these feelings could well disturb the system by which the child receives love and security.

The second consequence of this adaptation is the child's development of a false self. The child's sense of self is constructed of only those parts they know are safe to reveal to their caregiver, and over time these parts of self increasingly become who the child/person seems to be. They have masked particular feelings and needs from others and, most importantly, from themselves. As a result, they may feel empty and alone.

An inability to successfully separate from the primary caregiver is the third developmentally profound consequence of the child's adaptive situation. This separation process is called *individuation*. With healthy individuation, the parent helps the child to grow into independence and a secure sense of self, rather than an abiding interdependence or enmeshment with the parent.

A healthy person, according to Miller, is genuinely alive and has ready access to their true self and their emotional world. This person is aware of and able to be their true self. It is possible to heal and live in this way.

Miller highlights psychotherapy as a path to this healing. The psychotherapy process involves the individual first coming to understand what happened to them in childhood. This awareness and experiencing is accompanied by mourning what the person did not receive from the primary parent, especially in terms of acknowledgment, empathy, and acceptance of the child for who they are. Allowing these feelings can lead to acceptance and, ultimately, a new freedom and strength to be their true self: empathetic toward self, emotionally aware, honest, and articulate. They learn through this process to experience their own truth and recognize their own world of feelings.

DETACHING

Entanglements and You

FAMILY INFLUENCES: TRUE SELF VS. FALSE SELF

Take a moment to review the details of this past section about your true and false self as described by Alice Miller.

What has come up for you as you have
learned about the split-off self?

What feelings are coming up for you as you take in these ideas?

One of the things we understand about codependency is that it involves a pattern of looking externally rather than internally, of considering others more than self, of gauging self by the responses of others. Miller's description of the development of a false self explains how this other-directedness may begin.

As you work toward developing your healthy self—connecting with your true self—here are some questions to consider that can help to increase your connectedness with your internal life.

What are ways you limit contact with your feelings?

What are safe places and ways for you
to express your feelings?

What do you understand now about your
self that you did not know before?

How are you feeling about what you are
learning about your self?

Is there a split-off part of you that needs your attention?

Secure vs. Insecure Attachment Styles

Attachment theory was developed in the 1950s and '60s by John Bowlby, a British psychiatrist. The basic tenet of attachment theory is that an infant has an innate need to develop a relationship with at least one primary caregiver for healthy social and emotional development, and the patterns established in this primary relationship will be present in the child's future relationships. The infant has innate behaviors, such as crying and smiling, which stimulate innate caregiver responses from adults. The primary determinant of attachment is not food, but the responsiveness of the caregiver to the infant's behavioral signals for safety, security, and protection. This is called the *caregiver bond*.

Bowlby describes the specific dynamics of an infant/caregiver relationship that fosters a secure attachment. An infant becomes securely attached to an adult who is sensitive and responsive to their needs on a consistent basis. This attachment develops between the ages of six months and two years. Though the biological mother is often the primary caregiver, this relationship can be with anyone who takes care of the child over a period of time. Bowlby explains that in order to grow up mentally healthy, the child needs to experience a warm and intimate relationship with their primary caregiver, one that is satisfying and enjoyable for both.

The child's experiences with the caregiver create within the child an internal working model—a system of thoughts, memories, beliefs, and expectations about self, others, and the world. Emotions and behaviors are also cataloged within this system. This model is not just about what has happened to the child, it's also about the feelings that have arisen as a result of their experiences with their primary caregiver. This internal working model influences the attachment behaviors the child exhibits with the attachment figure. The child learns to anticipate and interpret the behavior of someone else and to plan a response. If the primary caregiver offers support and security, the child is likely to develop a positive image of self and what they can expect from others. If the child has received abuse, they are more likely to develop a negative image of self and expectations of others. This internal working model continues to develop over time, and has significant effects on the way the individual understands, interacts, and participates in various relationships over their lifetime. Though an individual's early internal working model may persist into adulthood, it is possible to make changes in it if the individual sees the need, is aware of their patterns, and is motivated to change.

In the 1960s and '70s, developmental psychologist Mary Ainsworth produced substantial observational research on Bowlby's theories about attachment. Working both with Bowlby and separately, Ainsworth validated the basic tenets of attachment theory, established the concept of the attachment figure as a secure base from which the child can explore the world, and identified three attachment styles in infants: secure, insecure avoidant, and insecure ambivalent/resistant. In determining these styles, Ainsworth was interested in the infant's behavioral signaling of their needs, as well as the sensitivity of the caregiver to those signals.

Secure attachment, A secure attachement style is characterized by the child's use of the caregiver as a secure base from which to explore and master their world. The caregiver has offered sensitivity, warmth, and consistency in their responses to the child's needs, and the child has experienced this. The child has learned that the parent is caring and trustworthy and can provide a safe haven for them that buffers against stress. This creates an internal security that gives the child confidence, comfort, and an ability to grow.

Insecure avoidant attachment style. This attachment style is characterized by the child's feeling that they have no attachment with the caregiver. They show no strong emotions upon being separated or united with the parent. The primary caregiver in this case has not been able to respond to the distress of the child. Emotionally unavailable, perhaps even to the point of rejection, the primary caregiver has likely discouraged crying and neediness and encouraged independence. The child's emotions have not been acknowledged, validated, and responded to. As a result, the child keeps their distance and may become rebellious. Their sense of self is low, as they have not experienced the caregiver as interested, caring, and attuned to them.

Insecure ambivalent/resistant attachment style. A child with an insecure ambivalent/resistant attachment style is not able to use their caregiver as a secure base. The caregiver has not provided consistent sensitive responses to the child. Rather, their responses have varied, ranging from appropriate to neglectful. The child feels anxious, as they do not know what to expect from the caregiver. They are preoccupied with the caregiver's availability to them, but often are reluctant to warm up to and engage with the caregiver when attended to and may even exhibit anger toward the caregiver in such a situation. This attachment style creates an anxious self that is preoccupied with the attachment figure but unable to establish a secure, predictable relationship with that figure or with their self.

Disorganized attachment style. In 1986, psychologist Mary Main identified a fourth attachment style in children: disorganized attachment. A child with this attachment style has no coherent way of coping. Their behaviors may be odd or disorganized. These attachment behaviors may well be in response to trauma experienced by the child or their caregiver. More on the effects of trauma on loss of self will be presented later in this chapter.

Attachment styles in adults. In the 1980s, attachment theory was extended to adult relationships (Hazan and Shaver, 1987). Several different assessment tools were created and tested to determine attachment styles in adults. Particular interest was in how the three predominant attachment styles identified in infants may present themselves in adult relationships. Bartholomew and Horowitz (1991) theorized and found through research using their Relationship Questionnaire (RQ-CV) that four adult attachment styles can be identified: secure, dismissive, preoccupied, and fearful. Their adult attachment model is based on the ideas that attachment styles are formed by thoughts the person has about others and about themselves. Does the person experience the other person as available, responsive, caring, and trustworthy? Does the person experience themselves as someone people want to respond to as worthy and loveable?

Briefly, these four adult attachment styles can be described in these ways. A **secure** attachment indicates the person is comfortable with both intimacy and independence. A **dismissive** style involves the person dismissing intimacy and being strongly independent. A **preoccupied** style involves the person being focused on a relationship and wanting it to be closer than the other person may be offering. A **fearful** attachment style involves the person being afraid of intimacy, wanting an emotionally close relationship but not trusting the other person to be there for them.

Understanding our attachment style(s) can be helpful as we get to know our self. Our relationship patterns may have been seriously influenced by our secure or insecure attachment styles. The more we know, the more we can change. Our internal working models about self and others can be changed if they are not working for us. Change involves becoming aware of your attachment styles and assessing how they are working for you now. This is best done with a mental health therapist who can provide a secure base for you as you explore your attachment styles and create new internal working models for your self.

DETACHING
Entanglements and You

FAMILY INFLUENCES: SECURE VS. INSECURE ATTACHMENT STYLES

Take a moment to review the details of this past section about secure and insecure attachments as described by Bowlby, Ainsworth, and Main.

What has come up for you as you have learned about secure and insecure attachments?

What feelings are coming up for you as you take in these ideas?

Relationships in which we act codependently often reflect an insecure attachment on our part. We cannot trust the other person, so we either hold on too tight or act strongly independent. We do not see our own worthiness and lovability, so we either over-function to keep the other person from leaving us or we live in fear of intimacy and won't let our self get close to others. An insecure attachment style contributes to an insecure sense of self and a vulnerability to loss of self in others.

As you work toward connecting with and cultivating your healthy self, understanding your attachment style(s) will be very useful. This can help you to understand your self better, see the patterns you may have in your intimate relationship history, and start making changes in you.

Do you see your self as having a secure or insecure attachment style?

If your attachment style is secure, consider what in your childhood experiences helped to create this security? Are you able to bring that secure self to your adult relationships?

If your attachment style is insecure, according to Ainsworth's descriptions of insecure attachment, are you insecure avoidant or insecure ambivalent? Or some of both? Specifically, in an important relationship:

How do you act toward the other person? What do you do?

What feelings come up for you in that relationship?

How do you feel about your self?

We can develop a secure self, over time and with good help. Safe, understanding, and reliable people, as well as places we can notice and accept our own feelings and our very self, are good seeds for this potential growth.

Individuation vs. Fusion and Homeostasis

It is instructive to think of our family as a system. In general, a system is an interconnected set of objects, people, or concepts that work together to create a product, an event, or a particular desired outcome. A heating system for a home is one example—in order to produce the desired heat, a number of interconnected parts all need to be functioning. Such is the family system from which each of us originates.

Murray Bowen developed the intergenerational family systems theory (FST), which explains this concept further. Patterns of relationship are learned within the family and passed down through the generations. Current individual and family behaviors reflect these generational patterns. The family system's goal is to maintain the status quo, to be homeostatic—regardless of the condition of that family system. This means that as one person within the system makes a change, changes are required of the others in order to keep the system fundamentally together. Stability of their system is the family's goal, and necessitates a balancing between the individuality of each of the system's members and a fusion to the family system. The main source of these family connections is the emotional nature of the individuals and the system itself. This emotional system guides, perhaps even drives, the behaviors, choices, and other social aspects of the relationships within the family system, including the formation of intimacy and identity.

Ultimately, healthy individuation from this family system is an appropriate developmental goal. It may also be thought of as differentiation of self. A differentiated person is able, even in the presence of their own anxiety, to be around people important to them and not feel responsible for, controlled, or limited by them. A person who has achieved healthy individuation has what the family system theorists call *personal authority*: having your own thoughts and opinions (as well as the ability to express them), trusting your own judgment, taking responsibility for your life experiences, choosing to be intimate with others, and experiencing your self as a peer to others, including your parents.

I have found it effective to illustrate these family system concepts using circles. These circle illustrations have become a way for me to teach the concepts and skills that foster a sense of the healthy, individuated self, one who can function both autonomously and within the various family systems of which they are a part.

RELATIONSHIPS

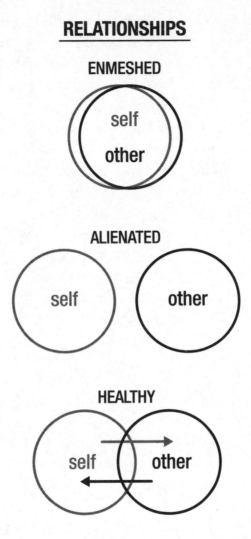

ENMESHED

self

other

ALIENATED

self

other

HEALTHY

self other

Consider each circle to be a person. In the first picture, the circles are overlapping, to the extent that there is little to no part of each that stands alone. The two circles, or people, are eclipsing each other. When these two circles are locked into this formation, we call this *enmeshment*. Neither person has a healthy, separate sense of self, and when either person attempts to separate, the other person reacts in a way to restore this level of enmeshment or fusion.

The second picture shows the two circles or people completely separate, with no shared selves. As was true in the first picture, these circles remain static. They do not change their basic relationship, which is to never come together in meaningful ways. We call this an *alienated relationship.*

The third picture shows the circles or people overlapping some, yet not completely. In this case, the individuals are able to both share themselves and keep a separate sense of self. We call this a *healthy relationship.*

This diagram of a healthy relationship does not remain static. Rather, it is dynamic, as the individuals are able to move toward or away from each other as needed and desired. Remember, each circle or person has its own boundaries. These two can intersect and cross each other as much as is *mutually* agreed upon. So the circles can range from almost completely overlapped to completely separate, depending on the expressed needs of each person and the mutual respect between them. This dynamic relationship allows for change and flow. It requires two individuals aware of their separateness and togetherness, and wanting to foster their self *and* their relationship in this way.

DETACHING
Entanglements and You

FAMILY INFLUENCES: INDIVIDUATION VS. FUSION AND HOMEOSTASIS

Take a moment to review the details of this past section about family systems.

What has come up for you as you have learned about how a family works as a system? Does this make sense in terms of your own life experiences?

Take in this concept of individuals within the system being challenged to individuate in the presence of strong emotions and bonds within the family system.

What feelings come up for you as you consider these ideas?

Developing a healthy self involves cultivating the personal authority described in this section. Codependence thrives in a family system that is threatened by you having your own thoughts, opinions, and feelings. You might also feel threatened by the possible consequences of being your self.

Though this work may take a long time, it is possible for you to develop personal authority *and* be a part of your family system. Both you and the system will change, simply as a result of your changes. Ideally, the changes in you will be centered in you and enable you to know your self, express your self, and have your self as your anchor and your own safe haven.

Considering the circle diagrams, how do you see your self in relation to your family of origin: enmeshed, alienated, or healthy?

What would you like your relationships
with your family of origin to be?

How well have you individuated
from your family system?

Are you able to be around family members without
feeling responsible for, controlled by, or limited by them?

Are you able to think for your self?

Are you able to express your thoughts and feelings?

Do you trust your own judgment, and are you
comfortable taking action based on your own judgment?

Can you take responsibility for your
own life experiences?

Family Rules and Roles

To help you look more specifically at the possible effects of your family of origin's influences on you, we turn now to the family rules and roles that held your family system together for better or worse and maintained the homeostasis necessary to contain the anxiety and other strong emotions present in your family system.

Claudia Black's work with children of alcoholics has provided solid and lasting information about these family rules and roles. In *It Will Never Happen to Me*, Black presents three primary rules contributing to dysfunction in a family: Don't Talk, Don't Trust, and Don't Feel. These rules dictate the way things operate in the dysfunctional family system. Although essential to the family system staying together and keeping some form of homeostasis, the rules are unspoken—even if that means a family member maintains an obvious addiction that profoundly affects others in the family. Don't rock the boat!

The Don't Talk rule means just that. Don't talk about what's really going on. Don't be honest. Don't express your concerns or feelings. Be quiet. Don't upset each other. Anxiety and fear fuel this one—it's better to be silent than risk disturbing the system. Guilt can come with violation of this rule. This rule causes a person to discount their own perceptions and to develop a high tolerance for inappropriate behaviors.

Don't Trust means that it is not safe to believe that another family member will really be there for you. It is not safe to share your thoughts and feelings with others in the family, as they may use them against you or not remember what you shared. It is not safe to depend on your parents for your physical and emotional needs, as they may not consistently provide these for you. This rule damages a person's ability to trust in other relationships over their lifetime.

Don't Feel means that it is not okay to recognize and experience your own feelings. Remember, these rules are about maintaining stability and consistency within the family system. By denying their own feelings and keeping their focus on others in their family system, a child is able to handle the inconsistencies of the family system and can cope. It is not safe to even recognize their feelings, so the child develops an internal system of minimizing or denying their feelings. This helps them to survive in that family system, but ultimately becomes problematic in many aspects of their adulthood.

In addition to family rules, family roles also are essential to the maintenance of the family system. As with the rules, the roles are not spelled out and assigned. Rather, children within the family system find their way to roles often (though not necessarily) related to their birth order and to their basic tendencies, as discussed earlier in Individual Influences. The taking on of a role can also be related to the unspoken needs of the family system at that time. These roles are designed for survival and protection and serve necessary functions for the child and their family system. The roles become problems, however, when the child becomes an adult and still operates in the role(s) they were wedded to as a child.

Black describes four roles (see Appendix A: Family Roles) in her book. These roles are The Responsible Child, The Adjuster, The Placater, and The Acting-Out Child. Studying these roles can help us see the role(s) characteristic of our self, and we can come to understand how we may be playing out these roles in our current entangled relationships.

Perhaps we are an organized, goal-oriented, self-disciplined person with difficulties in knowing how to listen, follow, let go, relax, and be flexible.

Perhaps we are easygoing and able to adjust to people and situations, but have difficulties making our own decisions and establishing a direction for our self.

Perhaps we are very sensitive to others, warm, caring, and giving, but have difficulties receiving from others and bringing a healthy focus to self.

Perhaps we are able to be very honest and just do things without questioning, but have difficulties expressing anger appropriately and following directions and rules.

Sharon Wegscheider-Cruse describes four other family roles (see Appendix B: Roles in an Alcoholic Family) in her book, *Another Chance: Hope and Health for the Alcoholic Family*. She presents four sibling roles taken on in a family: Hero, Scapegoat, Lost Child, and Mascot.

Perhaps we were the caregiver and are trying to be a caregiver in our entangled relationship.

Perhaps we sought attention in problematic ways and still do.

Perhaps we kept our distance in family relationships and now lack the skill sets needed to have a healthy intimate relationship.

Perhaps we were the funny, entertaining character and are trying to laugh and joke away our unhappiness with a relationship.

One other tool I find useful in helping clients to look at some of their earlier experiences that likely relate to their entanglements today is Janet Woititz's *Adult Children of Alcoholics*. This book broke new ground in defining a list of characteristics shared by adult children of alcoholics (see Appendix C: Characteristics of an Adult Child of an Alcoholic).

Although Woititz focuses specifically on the children of alcoholics, the material applies to the full range of family dysfunction. Anyone who grew up with dysfunction in any form—addiction to alcohol or other drugs, gambling, or overeating; chronic mental or physical illness; extreme and rigid religious attitudes; or who was adopted, lived in foster care, or in other potentially dysfunctional family systems—can identify with the characteristics Woititz describes.

Studying this list invites us to look at our own characteristics. Are we people-pleasers? Are we super-responsible or super-irresponsible? Do we need full control? Are we too serious? And how do these features of ours relate to our entanglements?

Perhaps we are entangled because the people-pleasing part of us believes we haven't yet done *the* right thing that will please the other.

Perhaps we are entangled because the super-responsible part of us believes we have not done enough, have not tried hard enough to make things work.

Perhaps we are entangled because we feel guilty when we do try to back off emotionally.

As we look at these roles and their developmental effects on us, remember that these roles in and of themselves are not bad. It's our rigid attachment to them that locks us in and keeps us from acting from our internal self. What we seek is the ability to listen to our self and to the situation at hand, then to choose our response from what we hear, rather than from old, external scripts written a long time ago.

DETACHING

Entanglements and You

FAMILY INFLUENCES: FAMILY RULES AND ROLES

Look at Claudia Black's family roles described in Appendix A. Mark the roles(s) with which you identify.

Look at Sharon Wegscheider-Cruse's family roles described in Appendix B. Mark the role(s) with which you identify.

Look at Janet Woititz's characteristics of adult children of alcoholics in Appendix C. Mark those characteristic(s) with which you identify.

Now, think of someone with whom you are entangled:

What entangles you with this person?

What parts of you make you vulnerable to an entanglement with this person?

Are you playing out any old, rigid roles with this person?

How do you feel when you are entangled?

How do you act when you are entangled?

Trauma

Over the past twenty years, both mental health and addiction services have come to recognize the importance of addressing trauma in the treatment of clinical symptoms. Trauma may be deeply embedded in someone who is depressed, anxious, or addicted. If the traumatic experiences are not acknowledged and addressed (when the person is ready), their healing will have its limitations. Beneath the surface of improved mood or reduction in addictive behaviors, the person may still be struggling with such symptoms as fear, shame, and insecurities.

As with each of these sections on Family Influences, the following will offer information in an introductory form. Trauma is an important area to consider as you learn about you and cultivate your growth. If you are interested in learning more about trauma, you'll find book titles in the Bibliography section of this book, as well as resources on the internet and at your local library.

Types of Trauma

Post-traumatic stress disorder (PTSD). We now understand trauma in several forms. Trauma is classically understood as experiencing actual death, serious injury, or loss of integrity of self, or witnessing these things, with resulting distressing patterns of symptoms that may involve reexperiencing the trauma and/or a numbing to protect self. These trauma symptoms may last months or years. We know this syndrome as post-traumatic stress disorder or PTSD. Some specific reexperiencing symptoms may include involuntary memories, vivid dreams, and flashbacks. Numbing symptoms may include avoiding people, places, and things that would remind the person of the trauma and refusing to think or talk about the trauma. Physiological symptoms may include being irritable, angry outbursts, being easily startled, and having difficulty concentrating or sleeping. Negative thoughts and feelings may well be present, including fear, anger, guilt, and shame. The person may develop distorted views about their self and others (e.g., "I am bad." "I am to blame." "People cannot be trusted."). They may have less interest in things they previously enjoyed, and may feel detached from others.

Relational trauma. Trauma does not have to meet all the criteria for PTSD to be a valid area of clinical work for deeper, fuller, and more complete healing. Relational trauma comes from the attachment wounds described in the Family Influences section on Attachment Theory. When the primary caregiver has not been sensitive and responsive, warm and attuned to the child on a consistent basis, the child may develop an insecure attachment style that may present with symptoms associated with PTSD. The child may be anxious and preoccupied with their primary caregiver or removed and emotionally detached. Other symptoms of physiological arousal and negative thoughts and mood may well be present.

These relational trauma responses have a physiological basis. During the first twenty-four months of life, the child's nervous system is developing. Bonding and attachment are essential to this neurological development—we are wired for love and relationships. When healthy development is thwarted by attachment wounds, automatic and reactive thoughts, feelings, and behaviors, directed at survival, are produced. We should keep in mind that these relational trauma responses are adaptive and protective; we know as well that they can limit optimum mental and physical growth of self, and the formation of meaningful and trustworthy relationships.

Complex trauma. Complex trauma generally refers to traumatic stressors that are interpersonal in nature. This is the trauma caused by one human who plans and carries out the violation, harm, or exploitation of another human. More specifically, these traumatic experiences have been repetitive and prolonged, have been perpetrated by primary caregivers or other responsible adults, and have often occurred during developmentally vulnerable times such as early childhood or adolescence. These events may also have occurred later in life to a person who is vulnerable due to disability, age, or illness.

Examples of experiences that may cause complex trauma include:

- Recurrent and severe physical abuse.
- Recurrent and severe emotional abuse.
- Sexual abuse.
- Chronic recurrent humiliation.
- Recurrent and severe neglect.
- Growing up in a household with:
  - Active addiction.
  - Domestic violence.
  - Mental illness.
  - Incarceration or hospitalization of a family member.
  - Absence of both parents.
  - Poverty.
- War/combat deployments.
- Refugee status and relocation.
- Sex trafficking.

The effects of complex trauma may include any of those associated with PTSD. Additionally, the individual who has experienced complex trauma may well experience specific symptoms, including difficulty regulating emotions, problems with attention, negative perceptions of self, identification with the perpetrator, mistrust of others, difficulty with intimacy, a broad assortment of medical problems, and a deep sense of hopelessness that they can ever be understood or relieved of their suffering. Complex trauma may cause prolonged feelings of helplessness, and a deformation of the individual's identity and sense of self.

Effects of Trauma

Understanding whether trauma has been a part of our life, and if so, what type(s) of trauma we have experienced, is a solid start to healing. To boldly name what has happened to us opens the door to greater self-understanding and self-compassion. Learning about the effects of trauma can help us understand more completely what is going on in and with us, and therefore know what we can do to not be constrained by the powerful effects of trauma.

Neurobiology. Trauma has a pronounced effect on our brain, and thus on the ways we think, feel, and function. We are very clear on this now. Though I have touched briefly on the effects of trauma on the developing brain in this chapter, the topic merits further elaboration here.

In terms of our brain structure, the limbic system is the emotional center. Located deep in our brain, it is the more primitive part responsible for our survival. It is the source of our fight, flight, or freeze reactive responses and regulates stress hormones, such as adrenaline and cortisol.

The neocortex is the more recently developed and advanced area of the brain. It is the center of thinking and reasoning. Our abilities to speak, to think abstractly, to reason, and to employ judgment originate from here. This area of the brain enables us to delay gratifications and to learn from our experiences.

Healthy operation of the brain involves the limbic system sounding the alarm, and the neocortex responding with reason and good judgment, producing healthy, balanced emotional and behavioral responses.

Trauma interferes with this healthy brain activity. Trauma causes the limbic system to be on high alert and to over-function, even when there is no impending danger. Unnecessary levels of cortisol and adrenaline are released, causing hypervigilance, reactivity, restlessness, fear, anxiety, worry, and stress. Trauma during the brain's developmental years causes the neurons in the limbic system to develop more densely, resulting in an even greater sensitivity to stimuli that trigger danger.

When the limbic system becomes more dominant due to trauma, the brain's capacities for reasoning and self-management—functions of the neocortex—are dramatically reduced. The limbic system and the neocortex stop communicating with each other, and the limbic system takes control.

Simply put, our healing incorporates quieting our limbic system and engaging our neocortex, so we can have a more balanced interplay between our feelings and our thoughts. Though this is a very challenging assignment, it is good to remember that this is what we are trying to do, so that we can calm down and find our own safe center to live in and grow from.

Functioning. Trauma interferes significantly with our functioning—at home and at work, in parenting, and in our relationships. When our brain is not functioning well, difficulties with emotional management and rational thinking can interfere with daily routines and responsibilities. Because there is a feeling of being unsafe or of things being unpredictable, it is not unusual to feel on guard and have difficulty proceeding with the normal activities of the day. A person may be preoccupied with trauma-based concerns, unable or unwilling to commit in ways necessary to make a job or relationship work. The structures of a "normal life" may be very hard to sustain.

Self. At the most fundamental level, trauma destroys self. By putting us on guard, trauma creates a foundation for external focusing needed for our survival if we are being traumatized, but not helpful to the development of self-awareness and self-consideration. When we are hypervigilant, constantly watching outside our self, we have no time, space, or brain for self. Psychologist Abraham Maslow, known for his hierarchical model of human needs, proposed that self-actualization—which is at the pinnacle of our needs—cannot be approached without a foundation of safety, security, and stability. Trauma can rob us of any and all of these basic needs. The result is that we have diminished:

- Connection with self.
- Self-awareness.
- Self-development.
- Identity formation.
- Self-confidence, belief in self.
- Self-expression.
- Comfort with self.
- Trust in self.
- Sense of self.

Thus, we see how self is compromised through traumatic experiences if we are unaware of this cascading potential, and not doing enough—as best we can—to keep at least a thread of connection with self, compassion for self, and well-wishes for self close at hand. With our limbic system in control, we lose our self to anxiety, shame, and anger, to sleeplessness, irritability, and agitation, and to helplessness and hopelessness.

Healing from Trauma

This brain science is a useful way to consider the effects of trauma and a useful structure for looking at healing. We want to be able to quiet the limbic system and increase our capacity to use the neocortex. We do not want our reactions, feelings, fears, and preoccupations to be so dominant. We want to be able to calm, connect with, and safely foster our self. We want to be able to think clearly, make healthy decisions, learn from our experiences, and trust what we know about our self.

This book is not about trauma treatment. A number of helpful books on the subject are available. This book is about loss of self, and to that end the content may help if you have lost your self as a result of trauma. You may find that you need deeper, more focused trauma work, and may do well to do that work with a mental health professional who can support, guide, and encourage you in a safe place and in safe ways.

The skills and educational material presented through the four areas of disentangle work can help in these ways:

Quieting the Limbic System. We can quiet our limbic system in a number of ways. We want to learn to bring our self to the here and now. Trauma often has our heads and hearts in the past. Cultivating present-moment awareness through regular practice can be calming, centering, and comforting, and actually helps to rewire our brains. You'll find details of how to develop these here-and-now practices in the section on Developing Spirituality—the first eight ideas on that list are about cultivating mindfulness practices that can help you become more grounded and relaxed, less judgmental, and more accepting of your self.

Activating the Neocortex. Reading this book is activating your thinking, learning, and decision-making capacities. Rather than spinning in your anxious, upset thoughts and feelings, you are settling your self enough to take in new ideas or revisit old ideas that you're more ready to consider today. Learning new things and developing your skill sets strengthens your neocortex. Learning to listen honestly to self, manage your feelings, and set healthy boundaries are such skill sets. New skills are needed to become more mindful and to cultivate spiritual practices. As you read further, you will be guided in your development of these skills— all of which can enable your brain to create new neural pathways that support lasting healing.

DETACHING

Entanglements and You

FAMILY INFLUENCES: TRAUMA

Take a moment to consider all that you have been reading about in this section on trauma.

How are you feeling?

What are you thinking?

What are you experiencing in your body?

Has anything come up for you relative to your personal experiences with trauma?

If not, that's okay.

If yes, that's okay. Try to just sit with that. This worksheet is about self-awareness, not about going into deeper work here and now.

Much has been said about the neurobiology of trauma, especially about the limbic system of our brain being too activated and causing disturbances in emotions, thoughts, and behaviors.

Do you often feel unsafe or on guard?

Do you feel stressed much of the time for unclear reasons?

Do you have emotional outbursts that are out of proportion to the situation?

> **Remember that healing from the loss of self that comes from living through traumatic experiences is greatly helped by quieting your limbic system and strengthening your neocortex—your brain center for thinking, reasoning, and relationships.**
>
> Are you ready to learn new things and develop new skills?
>
> Are you willing to try to think and act in different ways?
>
> Do you want to believe in your self?
>
> **Do you have a person in your life who would be an empathetic, understanding, and safe support for you as you make these changes?**

SOCIAL/CULTURAL/POLITICAL INFLUENCES

Having examined the Individual and Family Influences that may have contributed to loss of self in others, we now turn to the third ring of the diagram: Social/Cultural/Political Worlds. The purpose of this section is to increase awareness of ways you may have been influenced by the values, beliefs, norms, teachings, and actions of the world(s) in which you were raised.

As is true with this disentangle work in general, you are not being asked to change anything you socially/culturally/politically believe and live, unless you decide it's an obstacle to your personal growth. Your awareness of these influences is pertinent, but judgment of them and your self as you examine them is not part of this self-awareness process. Simply understanding your self better, and more fully, is the intent here.

Volumes could be written on this subject, as our world is full of various ethnic cultures, religions, and political systems under which people live. Differences abound in beliefs about gender roles and gender identity, the existence of a God, how people treat each other, how a country is best run, how to help the poor, how to manage a workplace, when life begins . . . You get the picture. We live in it every day—wherever we live.

The work here is for you to notice the things in your broader world that may not be true for you, that may be keeping you from speaking up, that may make you feel disrespected, or that negate you as a person. These are things that contribute to our loss of self, to our external, people-pleasing, conflict-avoiding ways. Here are a few examples of times and places this may happen:

- Are you restricted from something because of your gender? Your race? Your age? Your sexual orientation? Your income? Your religion?

- Are you asked to participate in social or religious activities that are not true for you?

- Do you feel like you have to participate in social conversations and activities that support gender roles and social status you do not believe in?

- Do the cultural traditions your family maintains feel uncomfortable for you?

- Do you feel like you are being treated as less than someone else?

- Do you feel like your time and needs are not being considered when you are asked to do things by others—at home, at work, at church, in an organization?

- Do you have no voice in your workplace? In the politics of your world?

- Are you being treated in ways that do not honor you as a worthy human being?

These questions are general things to consider, inviting you to be aware of your self as you move through your day with partners, family, work, church, social obligations, and government. You may find that one of these influences is really bothering you and contributes to how you feel about your self. You may find that one of these influences has contained you for a very long time, and you want to change that. The change I speak of here is a change in you, a change in the way you think, feel, and respond to the worlds in which you live. This is not about changing these large world influences directly. It is about helping you to find your way of living within and among these broad influences so that you feel respected and are being true to your self.

DETACHING
Entanglements and You

SOCIAL/CULTURAL/POLITICAL INFLUENCES

**Take a moment to consider what you just
read about the Social/Cultural/Political
Influences on your sense of self.**

Did any such influences come to mind for you?

Did the list of example situations prompt
any memories for you?

Are you currently living with a social/cultural/
political situation that has you feeling marginalized,
ignored, misunderstood, or uncomfortable?

Are you currently living with a social/
cultural/political situation in which something
is just not true for you?

**Imagine how you would like to be different with
that social/cultural/political situation:**

What are your feelings about you and that
situation?

What do you wish you could do differently for
and with your self in that situation?

What would you be saying?

What would you be doing?

How would you be feeling?

What will help you to make such a change?

Now that you have examined in some detail the question of who and what entangles you, and the sources of your loss of self, considering Individual, Family, and Social/Cultural/Political Influences, please read on for more self-education and skill-building to help you with your desired changes.

DETACHING
Separate Your Problem(s) from the Other Person's Problem(s)

When we are entangled, it can be very difficult to determine where we stop and the other person begins. We are mushed up together and stuck there. In both physical and emotional ways, there is little to no space between us.

So it should be no surprise that we take responsibility for things we are not responsible for, that we truly believe we know what's best for the other person, and that we allow our emotions to be so deeply affected by their moods and behaviors.

We are a tangled mess.

Mentally separating out the pieces of you from the enmeshed "us" is crucial to detaching. This means literally creating two separate lists: your problem(s) and the other person's problem(s). Now, as the twelve-step programs say, we're not trying to "take their inventory." We are not trying to solve their problems. We are, however, trying to surgically remove pieces of our self from this heap, so we can do something about our problem.

Too often we are taking way too much responsibility for our relationship working or not. Too often we personalize things the other person says or does, believing we are at fault, believing we are the one with the problem.

Learning to separate our issues and problems from theirs is essential to detaching. It allows us to see much more clearly what we can and cannot control in our relationship. It allows us to start seeing a self both in a relationship and separate from it.

DETACHING

Don't Try to Fix the Other Person's Problem(s)

A logical extension of separating our self and our problems from the other person's problems is letting go of trying to fix their problem(s).

Sometimes it is obvious when we are trying to fix someone else's problems. We try to stop them from drinking alcohol or using other drugs. We look for jobs for them. We take them to doctors, to counselors, to church.

Less obvious, but essentially similar behaviors might include such things as loaning them money, buying them clothes and possessions, and accepting excuses for their irresponsibility.

Even less obvious attempts to fix the other include efforts to cheer them up, efforts to motivate and encourage them, and efforts to keep them from being mad at us.

Sometimes we even try to fix problems of others that aren't really problems: "I bet you're cold. Let me turn up the heat." "I know you must be hungry . . . Here . . . Eat."

In our oceanfront hotel room one day, I said to my then eight-year-old daughter, "I bet you can't see out the window well enough"—it was a full-length, double sliding door—"let me get you a pillow." She had been just fine with her view. She didn't have a problem with it. *I* wanted her to have a "better" view. And how did I know what her view was anyway?

A good friend of my husband's helped me to see this fixing-other's-problems thing even more clearly. We were visiting his home in North Carolina. A bunch of us were headed downtown for some music. I was already in the car with our friend, waiting for my husband to join us. I said, "He seems to be in a bad mood, and I don't know what's going on."

Our friend matter-of-factly replied, "Well, if he has a problem he'll have to let us know."

What brilliance!

I heard him and heard him well. *He* didn't know the power of what he said, but that wasn't important. *I* knew.

This was a *great* idea: Let the other person speak up for their self!

We need to let others solve their own problems. We cannot solve them for them. They will have to do this for their self.

We have to let go of our belief that we can fix someone else.

We have to let go of our belief that fixing someone else will fix us.

We believe that if we can fix their problem, it will fix our problems. That is how entangled we are with them. Yes, some of their problem is in fact causing us some of our problems, but the resolution of their problem alone is not going to produce in us the serenity we desire. While it can be difficult to find contentment within ourselves, it is impossible to find it through others.

Let's fix our self.

DETACHING

Entanglements and You

**Think of someone with whom
you are entangled.**

**Draw two columns on a piece of paper
separated by a vertical line. At the top of one
column write My Issues/Problems. At the top of
the other column write Their Issues/Problems.**

**Fill in your column as best as you can. If you
stumble into items for their column as you
do your own, then jot them down under
the other person's column.**

**What are things you can do to work on
your own issues and problems as listed
in your column?**

**What are ways you try to fix their problem(s)?
Can you stop doing any or all of those things?**

DETACHING

Find Your Emotional Balance

When we are entangled, we often have almost no emotional space between our self and the other person. What they say and do dramatically affects how we feel and what we do. Their sadness makes us sad. Their anger brings on our anger or our regrets, apologies, and guilt. Their discouragement leaves us discouraged.

We react to whatever comes our way in our interactions with the other person. They've no sooner finished what they were saying than we jump in with our reactions and solutions. We sometimes don't even let them finish before we come running in with our response. And often those responses are intense, angry, or forceful: "You jerk! I can't believe you think that!" "I'm sick of you and your crap!" "That does it! I'm leaving!"

We are so emotionally close to the person that our reactions spin out of the web in which we are both entangled. If we have trouble seeing our self as a separate person with separate issues, it's no wonder we are emotionally tangled as well.

A brief look at what is going on with us neurobiologically at times of such strong upset can help us understand and employ the tools that follow. The intense feelings we are having, which prompt us to be so reactive, are based on physical things going on within our body at that time, more specifically, our autonomic nervous system that reads the situation and reacts. Here's what's happening.

Look at Appendix D: Illustration of Neurobiology and Self. I prepared this visual aid based on technical information about the autonomic nervous system, as detailed in Rick Hanson's *Buddha's Brain*, hoping to present it in ways easily received and understood by others. We have discovered a great deal about neuroscience and psychology over the past ten to fifteen years, and I believe it is beneficial for us to know what is going on in our body when we are anxious, stressed, upset, or lost. It can help us use our tools to calm down.

The hot water heater represents what is happening physically when we feel anxious and stressed. I incorporated it into the complete picture of a sink with faucets that can draw both hot and cold water into the basin of self.

When we are upset, our sympathetic nervous system kicks in and releases stress hormones, such as adrenaline, cortisol, and norepinephrine. At a low dose, these hormones are helpful in exciting and energizing us. At higher doses, however, they cause stress and worry and are responsible for our fight, flight, or freeze responses. This is a reactive system that protects us and is based in survival—the system works in reaction to things that alarm us and sets these stress hormones into action. Thus, out of the faucet connected to the hot water heater flows stress.

Out of the other faucet flows well-being. This side of the illustration is about the parasympathetic nervous system, which is in place to naturally calm us if our ways of thinking and feeling don't keep the reactive, sympathetic nervous system pumping stress hormones. The parasympathetic nervous system activates the signal for when danger has passed. It takes some minutes for the benefits of this system to become noticeable. Some of the biochemical benefits of the parasympathetic nervous system are the release of endorphins, natural opioids, nitric oxide, and dopamine. Where the sympathetic nervous system is *reactive*, the parasympathetic system is *responsive*, meaning it calms us so that we can think and act wisely, use our good judgment, and feel peaceful. I have used the image of a gentle, sunny day on the lake as a counter to the hot water heater. This lake reminds us to draw from such a calming image as we adjust the temperature of our stressed self. Yes, there are a number of things we can do to activate our parasympathetic nervous system, including relaxation, deep breathing, mindfulness, meditation, and imagery. Hanson elaborates on these ideas in very helpful ways.

Developing skills to move from a reactive to a responsive mode is what detaching is all about. When we practice these skills, we are quieting the fight/flight/freeze response of our sympathetic nervous system—the hot water heater—so that we can activate our parasympathetic nervous system—the calm lake on a sunny day. This neurobiological shift will allow us to achieve the emotional balance needed for our disentangle work.

Emotional balance enables us to see and hear the other person more clearly and listen to our self before we act (and not react).

We want to move from our old style of impulsive reacting to one of centered acting. We want to create the time and space to absorb what we are hearing from the other person and our self, and then, with both feet on the ground and our heart and head clear, offer to them our true and honest response.

It's not useful to simply give back to the other person what we think they want to hear. Nor is it useful to blast them with our anger and threats. It is even less useful for us to repeatedly apologize and throw our self at their mercy.

It *is* useful for us to emotionally center and process things before we respond. It is useful as well to make sure we are listening both to the other person *and* our self when we are deciding how to act.

As I have aged, my eyesight has gotten worse. In order to read words on a page without my glasses, I need to move the paper much further from my eyes. As I do this, the letters become clearer to me, the words appear, and the meaning of the sentences follows.

So it is with emotional balance. As we find that balance, we can see the person with whom we are entangled much more clearly. We can hear what they are saying and see the bigger picture. In so doing, we are more calm and centered, able to see and understand our situation with more clarity and meaning.

The following three sections offer specific ideas about how to achieve this emotional balance.

Observe the Other Person

**Observe the other person rather than fully interacting
with them, as loss of your self is likely if you do get
fully into the interaction with them.**

When I suggest observation, I have in mind a modified version of watching television, a movie, or a play. When we engage in these activities, we just sit back and take it all in. We listen carefully, often reflectively. We are not anxious to offer an immediate response to what we are hearing. Granted, we may be having reactions, even strong ones, but we keep them to our self as we absorb and process the stream of data coming our way. We are quiet, attentive, and thoughtful. We can be activating our parasympathetic nervous system by mindful breathing and being in the present moment. We can quiet our judgment and expectations, and simply allow our self to be aware of our feelings and thoughts as the external information is presented to us.

We do not jump out of our seats and react. Rather, we remain relatively centered, able to continue to receive and process what we are hearing.

My twelve-step program suggests that we adopt the evening news anchor's approach, simply announcing things in a matter-of-fact, reportorial style. I am suggesting that we also listen as though we were watching the evening news, with interest, objectivity, patience, and nonjudgment.

We do well to listen with an observer's stance that reminds us to not take what the other person is saying personally. The evening news is not personal. Neither is a lot of what someone else may be saying to us. Oh, we take it personally. We take many things personally. But really, what the other person is saying to us may in fact be more about them than about us. As we back off from the other, creating more physical and emotional space, we will be better able to see what is about us and what is not. We will see that we don't need to take it all personally.

It's when we take it personally that we lose our self in the interaction. At that point, we may jump out of our seats and react, unlike our behavior at the theater. We react and speak impulsively. We say things we don't mean and later regret. We talk in circles and repeat our forced points. Or our mind may go completely blank, and we can't move or think. Or we may run away with our upsetness. Our hot water heater fills us with those stress hormones, and fight, flight, or freeze is activated.

When my stress hormones are activated in this way, it feels like the floor has dropped out from under me and I have no ground under my feet. I am in free fall, grabbing for anything I can to convince, defend, defame, and control.

I can keep my feet on the ground and my self more centered if I work toward this observational style in a very conscious way. In my interactions with certain others, I have become aware of specific behaviors and ways of speaking that serve as warning signs to me, that I am about to hear something from them that may upset me in some way. When I notice this, I consciously remind my self to "Just listen. Stay calm. Observe. Think before responding. Don't feel pressure to answer their questions or requests immediately. Breathe. Stay with my self."

In addition to these cognitive-behavioral self-talk messages, we can do things with our body in these situations to help activate the parasympathetic nervous system so that we can observe. In trauma treatment, somatic therapies are often employed. These therapies involve becoming aware of bodily sensations and learning to regulate the self in response to these sensations. Meditation, yoga, moving to music, and walking are all forms of using the body to help healing from trauma by activating our parasympathetic nervous system to calm us when we feel stressed and reactive.

A specific body-based technique I suggest to promote this internal movement from reacting to observing is what I call emotional tai chi. In a confrontational interaction it is common for two people to be face to face with each other, their bodies also facing each other, sometimes quite closely as the interaction heats up. This posturing portrays the fight reaction and may even promote it as words, facial expressions, and gestures intensify. With emotional tai chi, rather than facing the person directly in such situations, I suggest we turn our bodies by around ninety degrees relative to the other person—so that we are still in the interaction, but what they are saying and the energy they convey, can move past us and not directly hit us and be absorbed into our being. This simple movement of our body, a mere sideways turn, can shift us from fight/flight/freeze responses to the possibility of hearing, thinking, and responding more effectively.

These strategies for centering our self—breathe, stay calm, shift your body, listen, think before responding—must remain conscious as the interaction proceeds. Staying connected to these strategies and using them helps to balance out the interaction, to avoid getting completely lost in the other person and what they are saying. I can feel my self creating emotional balance as I remind my self of these things and put them to use. I am creating a safety zone for my self that allows me to participate in the interaction and at the same time keep my feet on the ground, my head on my shoulders, my emotions under *my* control, and my spirit well and strong.

Act, Don't React

Act out of your centeredness and not out of your reactions to the other person.

I have been using the word "centered" throughout this book, but I am certainly not unique in suggesting that we find and operate out of our center. This concept is frequently emphasized in counseling and self-help worlds. Centered means that we are able to bring focus to our self and become stable and secure through that central, internal connection.

By disentangling, we are cultivating a self that is our center. Our self is the core of us. It is the heart of who we are, the place we go to listen to our thoughts, our feelings, and our needs. It is where we are aware of our physical, emotional, and spiritual lives.

When we have grown up people-pleasing, people-watching, and externally focused in general, we tend to be unaware of our self, our center. We may not even have much of a self. In my work, I often find that when clients have the opportunity to let go of thinking about what the other person wants, needs, or thinks, and instead think about their own wants, needs, and thoughts, they draw a big blank. They give me a very lost look, saying, "I have *no* idea what *I* want."

Some take this even further, explaining that without a focus on others, and without very straightforward feedback from others about them, they feel like they are not really there. They feel like they don't exist.

This can happen when we lose our self in others—we have no center from which to operate on our own behalf. We don't even think to factor in our self as we interact with the other person. As someone said in a meeting recently, "Where was *I* in the formula?"

Centeredness means that we return our focus to us, to our self. We can catch our self with our focus out there on others, watching for their reactions, their moods, their behaviors. We can catch our self trying to figure out what they are thinking or what they may need. And then we can turn those questions back to our self, asking what *we* are thinking and needing, watching our *own* moods and behaviors. This builds centeredness. Piece by piece, we cultivate that self by returning our focus to us and staying close to our self.

The feeling of centeredness gained by returning the focus to our self is generated and supported by our neurobiology. When I am centered, I simply feel better. My parasympathetic nervous system is in action, giving me a sense of well-being and helping me to a wise, calmly responsive mode. When I am *reacting* to someone or something, I feel off-center. My sympathetic nervous system is producing stress hormones like adrenaline and cortisol, and I am in a reactive mode. I want to act in extremes. I want to jump in and solve this problem now—and I mean right now!—or I may withdraw into sulking silence. When I am reacting, I am often impulsive in words or deeds, which I later regret and may spend much time cleaning up. I add guilt to my desperation.

When I act out of my centeredness, I feel more balanced and secure with my self. Though not necessarily relaxed, I do feel less stressed than when I am impulsively reacting. I am anchored by an inner calmness and clarity.

In situations where we find our focus is on the other, it is important to repeatedly pause and check in with our self. Ideally, we would not have left our self out in the first place. But many of us are starting out at square one with the development of our self. So we have to listen consciously to the other *and* listen to our self. If you have to take a break, in order to tune into your self and get back with the other person later, that's okay. In fact, that has at times been a very useful option for me, to get clarity and find my own voice.

Centeredness is having a self that we know, hear, foster, and stay close to. When I act out of my centeredness, I am including me in the formula. I am factoring my thoughts, needs, and feelings into the equation as I figure out the response I truly want to offer to the situation at hand.

Use Self-Talk

Use self-talk to help you when you feel pulled off your center (e.g., "I'm okay." "It's okay to say this." "I haven't done anything wrong." "This is not my issue.")

Self-talk means exactly that: talking to your self. While I imagine you've heard this may be a sign of questionable mental health, in this case I believe it can foster our mental health—assuming we are aware and rational as we talk to our self.

Self-talk is a technique used in cognitive behavioral psychotherapy. In self-help circles it often takes the form of affirmations. The technique can also be used to help disentangle. In each case, self-talk helps us to change the way we are thinking so that we are more honestly centered and anchored in reality.

When we are entangled, our thinking gets messed up. We become confused, frustrated, and lost. Our focus slips more and more onto the other person. We want to know what they think, what they are doing, and what they want.

When we talk to the other person, we try to say the things we think they want to hear. Or we say things we think may produce the results we desire. In any case, we are reacting to the situation, perhaps trying to manipulate the situation, rather than clearly and accurately representing our self.

Self-talk is about cultivating an internal dialogue with your self that may be as active as the external dialogue you are having with the other person. While you are talking to someone else, make sure to be checking in with your self as well, maybe even having an actual conversation with your self.

A brief example to illustrate: You have asked your partner if your family can spend Thanksgiving with your sister's family. You know that your partner disagrees with your sister on some topics, but she has invited you all to come, and you want to go. The conversation might go something like:

> **You:** "Jeanette has asked us to come for Thanksgiving Day. She'll fix the meal if we bring drinks and dessert. What do you think?"

> **Your partner:** "I think that I don't want to go. You should know that. We've been over this too many times already. I actually can't believe you would even consider going. What's wrong with you?"

At this point, you may already be feeling pulled off of your center; the hot water heater is kicking in. What you thought was a relatively straightforward question has quickly become fuel for an argument. You feel put on the spot to account for your behavior. Well, STOP for a moment to draw from your calming day at the lake and have a dialogue with your self.

> **Self:** "My partner is asking what's wrong with me. Do I think there is anything wrong with me right now?"

Self: "No, I don't believe there is anything wrong with me right now, except that I am feeling uncomfortable with this conversation and the way it is going."

Self: "Was I wrong to bring up this question?"

Self: "No, I was not wrong to ask about going to my sister's house. That is an okay thing to do. I want to go, and I'd like it if my partner would come also."

Self: "But I know that my partner is not nuts about my sister."

Self: "Yes, that is true, but I thought we could at least spend a few hours at her place without any big problems."

Self: "So what should I say now?"

Self: "Well, what is true for you now? What is it that *you* want to say to your partner at this moment?"

Self: "What is true is that I would like us to go as a family to Jeanette's for Thanksgiving Day."

Self: "Do you feel like you can say that to your partner?"

Self: "I guess so, but it sure makes me nervous."

Having a dialogue with our self can help us get in touch with our center. We ask our self questions about how we feel, what we need, and what we want. Self-talk helps us clarify things for our self and fortify our position. This fortification is not about fighting; it's about accurately representing *us* in a situation.

Self-talk can also be helpful outside of immediate interactions with others. We can use it to remind our self that it was okay to say or do what we did. Or to remind our self that we could not have done anything different in a past situation. We can use self-talk to bring our self out of our thoughts and worries and into the present moment. Self-talk can also help us prepare for future interactions that seem troubling and overpowering for us.

Self-talk is a way to find our center and a technique to help us stay there. In so doing, we create the emotional balance necessary for healthier interactions with others, and more stability and clarity for our self.

DETACHING
Emotional Balance and You

Think of someone with whom you have recently felt entangled. Perhaps you had an argument with them or were trying to get them to do something or to see something a particular way. Think of a specific interaction you had with them that demonstrates this entanglement.

With this incident in mind, try to practice these ideas for emotional balance:

OBSERVE

Thinking back on your interaction, try to see the other person as though you were watching them on a stage or on the television. Try to imagine your self sitting back and watching and listening to them. What do you hear them saying? How do they sound? What do you observe about their behavior? What are you observing about your self as you listen? What do you notice about your feelings? About your body? About your impulses to act or not to act? About your thoughts? Just observe.

GET CENTERED

Resisting the impulse to react to the other person in your usual way, pause and really tune in to all that you are observing. Make sure you are listening to you, as well as to them. What are you feeling, needing, and wanting in this situation? Find your balance by making sure you are focusing on both the external and the internal. What are you aware of feeling and thinking relative to this specific situation? Can you think of what you really want to do to act, not react in this situation? Or do you want to act at all at this time? Listen to you.

SELF-TALK

Go ahead and actually give your self a voice. What do you need to say to you about this situation? What are reminders that you need to say to your self so that you don't get lost in this interaction? What are the points that you want to hold on to, not to force them on the other person but to simply anchor your self? What are reassurances you can offer your self about you and your needs now? Talk to your self, and please listen to what you are hearing.

DETACHING
Be Aware of Your Motivations

Be aware of the motivations behind what you say and do in interacting with the other person. Make sure you are not saying or doing things to manipulate, control, or change them or to make them feel a certain way or do something specific. You are most likely to keep your centeredness if your motivation is to express your self assertively.

Being aware of what is motivating me to say and to do things is of the utmost importance. It took me a long time to realize this.

When I started on my journey, I had no awareness of how often I was trying to control or manage others. I had no awareness of my efforts to get the other person to do a wide variety of things that included liking me, doing things I wanted to do, and validating me.

And then through my own work, I began to see how tangled I would get entering a conversation with my own agenda, basically trying to manage or control someone else's feelings, reactions, or behaviors. I saw how I would repeat my points, say hurtful things, basically "throw in the kitchen sink" in my efforts to get the other person to do something or to even say they understood me.

Most of us don't like to think we are trying to manage or control others. Robin Norwood boldly laid this out as a characteristic of women who love too much. It was an eye-opener for me, and I've found it to be an eye-opener for my clients as well. Often when I first introduce to a client the notion of their trying to control someone else, they reject the idea. We like to think of our self as a sweet person, just trying to help.

But when we dig a little deeper, we find that we are not just "trying to help." We are deeply attached to making X, Y, and Z happen with the other person, and we are dead serious about it.

Becoming aware of our deeper motivations as we deal with others is a necessary step in helping us to detach.

The serenity prayer is a good tool to help us remember our own tendencies toward controlling and the limitations of what we really can and cannot control:

> *God, Grant me the Serenity to*
>
> *accept the things I cannot change,*
>
> *the Courage to change the things I can,*
>
> *and the Wisdom to know the difference.*

If my motivation is to try to change something I have no control over, I'm headed straight for an entanglement.

Once we are aware of our intentions, we can decide how we want to express our self. The basic recommendation here is to speak using "I" statements. Be as clear and direct as possible, and limit your attachment to the outcome of what you say.

Speak for *you*. Speak for what you believe and need to say relative to the situation at hand. Certainly, you may care about the outcome your speaking may bring, but don't get overly attached to it.

If a situation demands that a specific thing be done, well that's different, and needs to be handled with clear and meaningful expectations and limits. The following section on Setting Healthy Boundaries will provide many details about ways to express your self assertively and set necessary boundaries.

For now, understand that we can have greater detachment and fewer entanglements if we are motivated to speak for our self rather than with intentions to change someone else. We are separate people after all, with different views and styles. Knowing, seeing, and respecting our separateness and differences is paramount if we are to have healthy relationships.

With this separateness in mind, we can endeavor to speak up for our self, saying just how we feel and what we think. Doing so helps us to feel clearer, calmer, and stronger. And we tend to communicate a whole lot better, too.

DETACHING
Motivations and You

Think of a recent conversation you had with someone that you feel did not go very well. Perhaps you got angry or upset. Perhaps they did. Perhaps you simply felt bad about it after it was over.

What were you trying to communicate
in the conversation?

What were the motivations behind what you were
saying to the other person?

Were you aware of your motivations then?

Were you trying to change them in any way, or trying
to get them to say or do something?

Was this a situation where they absolutely <u>have</u> to do
or say something, or was that just your desire?

Did you get overly attached to the outcome
of the conversation?

Did you find your self saying a variety of things in a
variety of ways to produce your desired outcome?

Would the conversation have gone any better if you had:

Used "I" statements?

Been motivated more by simply representing your
own feelings and needs rather than pulling and tugging
at the other person?

Been less attached to the outcome of the conversation?

Understood and accepted that we are all separate human beings with different thoughts, styles, and outlooks, and we need to respect those differences rather than try to shape things in our own images and time frames?

"I don't understand how we get locked
into these arguments and can't unravel
them with love and caring for each other.
I get caught up in them . . . and I pursue
on and on like I really believe that's going
to eventually lead to where I want it to."

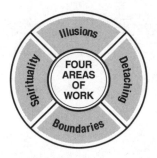

THE FOUR AREAS OF WORK

Setting Healthy Boundaries

Facing our illusions and learning how to detach can help us greatly with disentangling. Allowing our self to step back enough to see the reality of our self, others, and our situations can help us to stop being so consumed by the other person or situation. When we gain this emotional balance, we are able to see things more clearly and, hopefully, more accurately.

But facing illusions and detachment are often not enough to leave us feeling we have a strong, clear, and healthy self. They are essential starting points for disentangling and cultivating a healthy self, but we also need to set boundaries.

This need for boundaries became clear to me in my work with a client some years ago. She had initially come to me because her relationship with her husband had left her feeling confused and inadequate. In their interactions, she usually felt like she was wrong or had done something wrong. Through her counseling work she learned not to fall prey to this response, but rather to detach, observe, listen, and process things for her self. She started to see more clearly what her part in their problems was and was not. She started to feel better.

But one day she called me with an emergency. She'd had a major argument with her husband and was feeling lost again. The argument had been over her accountability to him. He was angry because he had called her from his out-of-town job, and she wasn't home when he called. They'd had no agreement about a calling time. Her husband accused her of cheating on him and demanded that she stay home all the time to be available for his calls. Further, he insisted that when he returned she make no plans other than to be available to him.

We talked about this situation. My client was able fairly quickly to find her detachment skills and get a better look at what had happened. But she still felt bad, angry, and hopeless. It was clear that for her continued growth, and for the health of this relationship, she really needed to start setting some reasonable boundaries for her self. Now that she could see things more realistically, she could start doing this. She needed to learn that it is okay to set boundaries. She needed to figure out which of her husband's demands she would meet and which she would not. She needed to learn how to assert these boundaries and stick by them. She was clearly into the next phase of her growth.

So what does this "setting boundaries" entail? Setting boundaries does not mean establishing walls that cut us off from others. Nor does it mean rigidly attaching our self to rules and procedures that don't necessarily apply or work in all situations.

Setting boundaries does mean establishing some limits for your self regarding what you will and won't tolerate in a particular situation. Setting boundaries means that you are able to listen to your self, know your limits, and firmly assert those limits to your self and the other person.

Setting boundaries is really a healthy, friendly thing to do. It helps us to know the parameters of our relationships and interactions. Without letting someone know what your boundaries are, how are they to know what is and is not okay with you? It would be like playing a game without first establishing any rules. What a chaotic mess that would be! The game would likely go nowhere, and efforts to play it would surely end in frustration and anger.

So it is with our interactions with others and with our self. Our children need boundaries and limits. So do the adults with whom we interact. And we often need to set limits with our self. How often have you taken on more work than you should have or wanted to? How often have you said, "yes," when you really wanted to say, "no"? Have you ever overspent? Overeaten? Overelaborated? Overgiven? Overimbibed? Do you ever disregard time or your physical or emotional needs? Do you ever disregard the limits set by someone else relative to what they need and want from you?

All of these are daily manifestations of the need for boundary setting. We are given many opportunities to practice setting and keeping limits that help us to be healthy and strong individuals and thus, more capable of healthy relationships.

But setting limits does not come easy for many of us. Some of us have had no practice at all. We have never even entertained the idea of setting a limit. Others of us think we have set boundaries, but have really just been trying to manage and control the behavior of others. Our focus has been on what we think others need their lives to be like, rather than on what limits we need to set for our own lives.

Even once we know what boundaries we need to set, stating them is hard. All sorts of fears arise, including the fear that the other person will not tolerate the limits and leave or the fear that we are just wrong to take the stand we think is right for us.

Our task then is to stick with the limits we have set. Setting boundaries and then not following through with them undermines our efforts to establish our self. When we set a limit with someone and don't stick with it, the other person learns to not take us seriously. They know we really aren't going to do anything if they don't respect our limits, and so the chaotic game continues, while frustration and anger mount.

Setting boundaries for our self and with others is necessary, but can be difficult. This section will present some of the basics of how to set limits. The ideas are directed at helping you listen to your self more carefully and fully, to successfully communicate to your self and to others what you will and won't accept, and what you will and won't do. These ideas will help you find and keep your center as you assert and enforce your boundaries.

SETTING HEALTHY BOUNDARIES
Slow Down

It is so easy to simply react when we are angry, anxious, confused, or disappointed. We want to impulsively blurt out our feelings and thoughts without thinking. And we do.

In order to disentangle, however, we need to slow this process way down.

We want to move from reacting to acting. And in order to act, we need to be centered and aware of what is being said, and what we want to say back.

So when you're in an interaction with someone and feel your self start to lose your balance, slow down. Create some time and space between what the person says to you and how you respond. This is where we remember the neurobiology going on within us as these disturbing interactions happen. This is where we remember to activate the calming parasympathetic nervous system and not just keep the hot water heater boiling (see Appendix D).

There's a lot of wisdom in the old prescription to count to ten when upset. But rushing from count one to count ten in order to go ahead and blurt out your slightly delayed response is not what I have in mind here.

A better approach is to mindfully bring your focus to your breath, following that for several counts. Perhaps ten slow breaths would be good. And while you are doing that, maintain focus on your breath, not on what you are just dying to say to the other person.

The object is to take a momentary break so that you can collect your self. That includes your thoughts and feelings, needs and wants.

We are slowing down the interactions here, so that the communications we make are not based on habit, impulse, or reaction. Rather, this slowing down increases the chances that you will more effectively communicate what you mean. You will keep your feeling of centeredness and not have to run around apologizing and explaining your self for days after.

When I am centered and in good form, I can sometimes anticipate moments in my interactions with others that stand to upset me or, at least, disturb me. When this happens, I consciously tell my self not to respond right away to what the other person may say. I tell my self to simply listen to them, hear them out, and then intentionally pause and calm my self before I proceed.

Sometimes in such a situation, I can't proceed until I take a break from the interaction. For me this may mean taking a walk outside or going to another room for a while. For others, a break may mean journaling, talking to a friend, reading, or any number of pleasurable outlets that refresh us and help us figure out how we do want to respond to what has been said or done to us.

It's okay to take this type of break. Generally, we don't have to give the other person a response right away. We may want to, or feel like we have to, but often we don't. So, take the time you need to respond in the way that best represents you.

Whether we slow down our interactions by minutes, hours, or even days, the point is that in order to speak for our true self, we need to make sure we are not caught in the tentacles of a bad interaction. When we are caught this way, we are on the defensive and struggle to free our self in random and aggressive ways. We may even send our tentacles out to entrap the other person.

Slowing down our reactions enables us to slide out of the way of the tentacles, leaving us free to clarify what we truly want to say, and to assert it in a way that is respectful of both the other and our self.

SETTING HEALTHY BOUNDARIES
Listen to the Four Areas of Your Self

It is easy to narrow our focus onto the other person when we are angry, anxious, confused, or disappointed. As an interaction becomes more intense, those of us prone to entanglements become increasingly riveted on what the other person is saying, how they look, and what they are doing. We lose our self in this way.

When we are completely absorbed in listening to the other person, we cannot listen to our self. In order to disentangle, we need to bring our focus back to our self. This is the heart of my message here. In the space we create for our self by slowing down, we can listen to the voices within us that help us know how we want to respond. Those voices originate from four areas of self: our mind, our feelings, our body, and our spirit. In the diagram below, each circle represents an area of self, and the intersections of these circles show the integration of these aspects of self that becomes possible as we listen and respond to self.

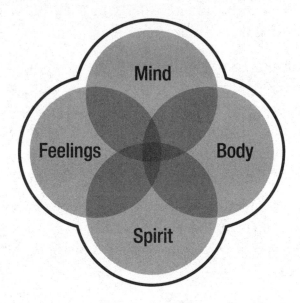

The voice of our **mind** can tell us what we think about this situation. It can tell us what is logical, fair, appropriate, and acceptable to us. Our mind reminds us of our position relative to this situation, which we perhaps quickly lost track of as the interaction took off. Our mind can help us sort through the pertinent variables, organize and evaluate those variables, and plan some course of action.

But to hear only the voice of your mind will not give you the full picture about your self; the voice of your **feelings** must also be factored in. How do you feel about this situation? About the person involved in this interaction? How do you feel about how you are treated? About how you treat your self relative to this person and situation? Are you okay with things as they are? Do you need something to be different? How do you feel even asking your self these questions?

The voice of your **body** has many messages for you as well. By voice of your body, I mean your physical self. How do you feel physically? Are you aware of stress, tension, chronic pain, or illness? Do you have physical complaints that you ignore? How does your body feel when you are caught in an entanglement? What does it do? Does your body move toward the problem, away from it, or is it paralyzed? Many years ago, I read a suggestion that has been meaningful to me and applies here: When you can't figure out what you think or feel, notice what your body is doing. Our physical self has a lot of relevant information for us.

And the voice of our **spirit** is equally important, though too often it is disregarded as we forge ahead into our entanglements. The voice of the spirit is the opposite of our forcing solutions. It may be our gut feelings, intuitions that are strong and clear yet defy easy explanations. It may be our contact with a power greater than our self, by which we let go of our tight hold on a situation and allow things to unfold on their own. The voice of our spirit may be a quiet mindfulness that rests our mind and our feelings, allowing pieces to come together in ways we could never imagine on our own.

Listening to our self means hearing *all* of these voices and not jumping to conclusions or actions based on none or one or two of them. If we don't listen to all of them, we are not being fair to our self. We are making perhaps consequential decisions based on inadequate information.

Granted, as we listen to these voices, we may find some conflict among them. Logic may tell you to leave, while your heart says stay. Everything may be working out well in your relationship, but something tells you it's wrong to be in this relationship. As we listen to these conflicting messages, we need to respect them all and weigh them against each other as best we can to determine where we stand and what we need to say or do, if anything, right then. Maybe all we can say in such a moment is that we are very confused and we'll have to get back to the other person when we have more to say.

It is pretty amazing how much information about our self is right here with us all along. We just have to make sure that we tune in to each of these areas of self and patiently listen to what our mind, our feelings, our body, and our spirit are telling us.

SETTING HEALTHY BOUNDARIES
Respond to the Four Areas of Your Self

On the topic of relapse prevention, twelve-step fellowships recommend a most helpful acronym: HALT. This stands for Hungry, Angry, Lonely, and Tired. If we are dealing with any or all of these states of being, we become vulnerable to regressing to our weakest link. With substance addiction, the regression is the use of addictive substances. With addiction to activities, this could mean a return to pornography, spending, eating, or gambling. With codependence, it can mean the loss of self in someone else. Setting healthy boundaries is dependent on our HALTing and taking care of what needs to be tended to first for our self.

This tending to self requires not only listening to the four areas of self, but responding to them as well. Tending to our self in each of these areas can foster our centered self, which is responsive, not reactive. This may take a while. The ideas and examples offered here are to point you in the direction of good self-care, and to help you see the relevance of doing so as you move toward healthy boundary setting. For a simple example, if you are tired, you should go to bed and get good rest before you try to figure out the boundary you want to establish. Here are some ideas in each of the four areas of self.

Mind. If our mind is confused or caught in a negative cycle of thinking, we do well to do those things that calm and center us, so that we can access clearer and more rational thoughts. Once we can think more clearly, we can use self-talk to correct our distorted thoughts fed by anxious feelings. We can remind our self of what is real and true. We can remind our self that we are okay and can trust what we are thinking and doing. We want to cultivate a friendly relationship with our mind, not let it run away with us. We want to notice the messages it relays and the ruts it gets into that bring us down and make change difficult. Setting healthy boundaries requires a cleared mind that is able to problem-solve and decision-make with good judgment and confidence in self. Taking time to access this clearer, centered mind is essential and may take both time and a deep willingness on your part to interrupt the patterns and messages you keep telling your self.

Feelings. We can do a number of things with our feelings, but we have to first become aware of them. For some people, their minds are more dominant than their feelings, and they have to intentionally shift to awareness of their feelings. For others, their feelings may be more dominant than their thoughts, and they can help themselves by managing their feelings to think more effectively. In either case, working with feelings requires becoming aware of and identifying them.

Feelings are signals to us. They can be strong, disturbing, and often misdirected; they can be healthy releases of tension and unhappiness as well. In whatever ways they may manifest, it is not uncommon to be uncomfortable with feelings and not know what to do with them.

The flow chart in Appendix E: Chart for Healthy Emotional Expression, gives us a picture of various things we can do to manage and respond to our feelings. Briefly, here are those ideas:

1. **Chaperone/Be with our feelings**: This is based in the practice of mindfulness described by Thich Nhat Hanh. It involves learning to recognize your feelings and simply be with them, breathing mindfully and holding those feelings as you would hold an infant. Not judging the feelings or trying to do anything with them, but instead just being with them.

2. **Cues/Signals:** This means noticing your feelings as information for you about you. Are the feelings you have signaling your need for improved self-care? Are your feelings signaling your need to HALT? Our feelings, if we are willing to listen to them, can be ready cues to stop, regroup, restore, and collect our self.

3. **Contain:** Learning how to contain our feelings is critical. Contain does not mean to push feelings away or hide them. It means bringing them out to express, examine, and work toward some resolution, and then setting them in a place where you can leave them and return to them as you wish. You develop the ability to not be carrying these feelings around with you all the time, having them bleed into people and interactions in destructive ways. You might try a number of different ways to contain feelings, including leaving them in your journal, in a drawer, on a shelf, or in your counselor's office.

4. **Communicate:** We certainly want to be able to communicate our feelings when we are able to. It is useful to first practice expressing your feelings to

safe people. These are people you feel are willing to understand you and not make you feel bad for whatever you want to share, people who will not judge you or tell you what to do. They will understand the healing journey you are on and empathetically listen to you.

We also want to develop the ability to speak up to the person involved in our strong feelings. Many of us are conflict-avoiders, and speaking about our feelings with the other person can be scary. This is where assertiveness comes in. Being assertive is its own skill set, the basics of which I describe in Appendix F: Continuum of Expressive Behaviors. This diagram shows the range of behaviors, from passive to assertive to aggressive. Assertiveness, in the center, is our ability to express our self in the form of an "I" statement, with tones that are respectful of both our self and the other person. If we are not careful as we work to assert our self, we may shift on the continuum toward either passivity or aggression. Self-awareness and practice can help us remain assertive as we express our self.

5. **Change your neural structure:** As previously discussed, our neurobiology contributes to our strong feelings, but can also be adjusted to help us manage and achieve some closure with them. As we quiet the hot water heater of our sympathetic nervous system and access the sunny day at the lake of our parasympathetic nervous system, we are actually creating new neural pathways, channels that can move us from a negativity bias toward positivity. Allowing good experiences and feelings to seep into our self, we help to change our brain structure in ways that promote more balanced emotional experiences, rather than living with the fight/flight/freeze response ever close at hand.

Body. Let's go back to HALT. We've covered ways to respond to feelings such as Angry and Lonely before acting. Now let's consider Hungry and Tired, both physical states that ask us to take care of them before we do something unhealthy to our self— or before we try to set effective boundaries. If we find our self irritable, too tired or hungry to think, or it is too late at night and we need to go to bed, we should heed these body messages and act on them before boundary setting. Similarly, if we have a medical issue we have not addressed, we should schedule an appointment so we can understand and treat our symptoms. If we are stuck on the couch, we should get up and move; if we want to get a massage, we should. If our kitchen cabinets are full of unhealthy foods, we should go to the farmer's market. Our body is full of information for us, and our attending to the messages it gives will help us feel better, think more clearly, and thus figure out our boundaries more readily.

Spirit. Responding to our spiritual self can be lovely. We can let go of forcing solutions and allow things to unfold as they will. We can do our part and let go. We do well to listen for the inner voice of our spirit that invites stillness, quiet, and space, that part of us that trusts that we are not in full control and that a power greater than our self may well be in play. Perhaps the spiritual area of our self needs more attention and consideration and to be called upon more often. If you find the circle of spiritual self less prominent than the other circles of self, it might perhaps be expanded through a willingness to cultivate practices that support your letting go of things you cannot control.

SETTING HEALTHY BOUNDARIES
Use "I" Statements

We can readily start pointing our finger at the other person when we are angry, anxious, confused, or disappointed. In a heated situation, often the first word out of our mouth is "you":

"You never do what you say you're going to do!"

"You do the same thing and more of it!"

"You have a problem and just don't want to face it!"

"You're a jerk."

"You make me sick."

"You're the one who got us into this situation."

"You're always _____."

"You're never _____."

Starting our statements with "you" tends to put the other person on the defensive *immediately*. When someone says "You . . ." to me, my gut response is to account for, explain, and defend my self, and I'm ready to argue about this statement about me rather than address whatever topic we were trying to discuss.

"You" statements feel very personal and solicit very personal responses often loaded with emotion, with an extremely narrowed focus. Our focus shifts to protecting our self against what feels like an assault, and may well be. We need to defend our very self from this bombardment.

In order to disentangle, I find it much more useful to start statements with "I" when I am engaged in an intense and conflicted interaction:

"I am disappointed that you have changed your mind."

"I am angry that this work did not get taken care of."

"I am not happy living in this situation. I need to make some changes for my self."

"I don't know what to say right now. I am confused and very angry. I'll get back with you later."

"I am worried about you. I miss how it used to be with us."

"I really wish you would go there with me."

Starting statements with "I" helps to create a climate where we can continue to discuss things. To this end, "I" statements contribute to disentangling. They are simple, clear statements to the other person of what's going on with you and where you stand.

In order to make an "I" statement, you have to stop and think about how you are feeling and what you want. Sometimes this is a real challenge. As these intense and unproductive interchanges progress, we get further and further from the original point. "I" statements help us anchor our self back to what we wanted to say in the first place.

Similarly, "I" statements reduce entanglements because they are not putting the other person on the defensive. "I" statements to the other person offer them clear information about you and do not challenge the other person's sense of self. They can have a steadying impact on the conversation at hand.

I find "I" statements to be clarifying and anchoring. They help me re-center my self to not make a difficult situation worse. And I often find that "I" statements help me start finding the path out of an entangled interaction.

SETTING HEALTHY BOUNDARIES
Make Statements Rather than Ask Questions

Questions can be okay. Then again, they can be a problem if their purpose is to manipulate or control the other person or situation:

"Have you asked off from work yet?"

"Do you know when you are going to ask?"

"Have you even thought of how you're going to do it?"

"You are going to ask aren't you?"

"Have you finished that report yet?"

"When do you plan on doing it?"

"Don't you think you should stay home tonight and work on it?"

"Aren't you worried about getting it done?"

These sets of questions are examples of how we get on a roll as we try to get another person to do what we think they should be doing. The effect of such questioning is profound.

Notice the number of times "you" appears in these questions. Whether "you" is used in statements or questions, the result is essentially the same: the other person is on guard and the chances of effective communication are pretty much shot. The person being questioned feels attacked.

The person asking the questions is generally not having a very good time of it either. With our questions, we are usually after some specific answer—and this type of "questioning" doesn't tend to produce that answer. So we get more and more frustrated and ask more and more questions. And we get angry and lost.

If we stop and think about what we want to say to the other person, we can usually make a statement that conveys our true intent behind this wall of questions:

> "I am really hoping we can go on the trip we are planning."
>
> "I'll be glad when you know if you can get off from work for that time."
>
> "The sooner you can find out, the better it will be for me and the other arrangements I need to make for the trip."
>
> "Please let me know as soon as you find out about getting off from work."

> "I'm worried that you are not going to get your report done on time."
>
> "If you need something from me that will help you get going on it, let me know."

These statements more clearly express where I stand and what's going on with me relative to the other person. They help both of us to know what we are trying to say, rather than dragging the other person around with questions that carry implied meanings and hints.

Statements to the other person give us a foundation upon which to stand. That foundation is built on our clarity of thought and the emotional centeredness that comes from asking our self questions about how we feel and what we want and then taking those answers and expressing them as statements to the other person.

SETTING HEALTHY BOUNDARIES
Set and State Your Boundaries

This disentangling idea comes in two steps: setting boundaries and then stating them. Don't try to do both at the same time. Don't state your boundaries out loud as you are figuring them out. They may not be what you really mean and want.

> "If you don't ask for that time off today, I'm divorcing you."

> "If you don't complete your report tonight, I'm selling your car."

Instead, first decide for your self what your boundaries are. Using your skills of slowing down and listening to you, you can figure out:

- What you will and won't accept from the other person.
- What you will and won't do for them.
- What you can and cannot offer them.
- What your limitations are in terms of time, money, and energy.
- How much you can physically and emotionally invest in the situation.
- What would be the best for you in this situation.

These are not necessarily easy questions. Often we don't know the answers immediately. So how do we find the answers if they don't come to us right away?

Well, while we are considering what the other person has asked of us, we look at our schedule, we check our finances, we consider what we have on our own list of things we need to do.

While we are thinking about what the other person said or did to us, we need to notice how we are feeling, what we are needing, and what we are doing.

We can take all the time we need to set our boundaries.

We want to make sure our boundaries feel right to us.

And then, once we have figured out our boundaries and are comfortable with them, we let the other person know what they are, stating them simply and with ownership:

> "I cannot go on the trip if I don't know your plans by Friday."

> "I will not call for our reservations until you tell me when you can get off from work."

> "I am going to make my own reservation for my flight. I'm leaving it up to you to make yours once you know your work schedule."

> "I need to work on the computer tonight for a couple of hours starting around 9:00 p.m. I just wanted you to know so you can plan your work on your report around that."

> "I've asked you enough about your report. I'm not going to bring it up again. It's up to you to take care of it."

Easily said, easily done, right? No. For many of us, boundary setting is not so easy. It is hard to set boundaries, often even harder to state them to others, and harder still to stick with them. Many of our people-pleasing, conflict-avoiding behaviors take center stage when we try to set limits with others.

We are so afraid of upsetting, inconveniencing, disappointing, or angering others that we only reluctantly approach boundary setting. Guilt gladly steps in to make our assertive behaviors even more difficult, if not impossible at times.

So with these personal obstacles in mind, the following additional ideas about Setting Healthy Boundaries are offered to help us maintain our strength, clarity, and centeredness as we present our boundaries to others.

SETTING HEALTHY BOUNDARIES
Stick with Your Limits

When we first state a boundary, we may feel strong and sure. Give us a few minutes, hours, or days, however, and we're either backing down from what we said or pretending we never set the new boundary at all. It is easy to not follow through with the boundaries we set.

It should come as no surprise that we have trouble sticking with our limits. A quick glance back at the characteristics of adult children of alcoholics described by Janet Woititz (see Appendix C) will remind us of a least some of the reasons:

- Our fears of abandonment allow us to believe that if we stick by our limit with another person they may leave us.

- Our needs for constant approval and affirmation are thwarted by limit setting, as the other person often does not approve of our new decisions.

- Our super-responsibility may convince us that if we follow through with this limit, whatever we believe needs to be taken care of may not get done, so we need to go ahead and do it anyway.

- Our loyalty may instill in us the belief that we are not being fair to the other person and that we need to stick by them in our same old ways.

- Our needs for immediate gratification are also thwarted. Though the limit setting may in the long run improve our situation, at first it may not bring the gratifying results we seek. In fact, it may leave us feeling even worse than before.

And then there is plain old guilt. We may feel guilty because we are "doing this to them." We feel bad about saying "no." We feel bad about looking after our needs. Guilt moves in like a weight upon our chest and heart. It sings its song in our ear. Guilt makes it very hard to stick with our limits.

In order to disentangle, we need to stick with the boundaries we've set. If we don't, we stand to continue the tangled games in which we are caught.

We will be sending the message that we really don't mean what we say. We will be telling the other person that, though we were upset at the time, we can get over it and accept things as they usually are. What we are really saying is we don't respect our self enough to enforce what we've decided we need.

At worst, we go back and apologize for the boundaries we set, ask the other person to forget about them, and then try to make up to the other person. This encourages the old tangled ways. And my own experience is that I feel pretty horrible again fairly quickly after discarding or discounting my boundaries.

So how do you stick with your boundaries? Use your self-talk. Keep reminding your self of how and for what reasons you set these limits. Become a broken record, keep repeating your boundaries if they are being challenged. Remind your self of what will happen if you don't stick with your limits, of how miserable you'll feel if these new limits are not enforced. Remind your self that people notice when you do not do what you say, that this is what you need to do for you, and that it's okay to make a decision like this with your self in mind.

You may have to learn to sit with your guilt; it does not automatically go away with these reminders. You may have to sit with the discomfort that comes from the disapproval you receive and the conflict you experience.

In order to make real changes that untangle us, we need to go through the uncomfortable feelings that come with doing things differently, with the belief that stating and sticking with our limits will help us eventually to interact with others in healthier ways. And we can, sooner or later, begin to feel better, too.

SETTING HEALTHY BOUNDARIES
Say Things Once

There's a lot to be said for brevity.

Saying what we need to say, then stopping, has real strength and cleanliness. It conveys that we know what we are talking about and are sure of it. It can also have a matter-of-factness about it that says, "I'm not making a big deal over this. This is just where I stand."

Saying things once can be difficult. We tend instead to repeat our self in a variety of ways, for a variety of reasons.

We repeat our self by bringing up the topic again and again. We repeat our self by explaining further and further what we mean and why we are doing what we are doing. We repeat our self when we say, "Do you understand why I am doing this? Do you understand what I am saying?" And when we decide we've not made our self clear to the other person and need to say the same thing in twelve different ways—well, you get the picture.

Why all of this repeating? Another glance at Woititz's characteristics of adult children of alcoholics suggests a number of possible reasons. We are uncomfortable with the change our new boundaries will likely bring. We are afraid the other person will leave us. We don't like the disapproval we may be receiving. We are starting to feel responsible for this whole mess.

So we overstate our case, hoping the other person will come to some eventual understanding and say to us, "I know exactly what you mean, and I think you're doing the right thing by setting this limit with me. I love you dearly for it, and I will never leave you."

But repeating our self is not likely to produce such a result. In fact, going over and over a topic often antagonizes both parties, serving only to confuse and dilute the original point.

So once I am ready and able to state my boundaries with someone else, I find it useful to say it only once. Granted, sometimes clarification may be needed. But beyond that I need to pay careful attention to any impulses I may have to say more about the limit I am setting. Usually these impulses come from my own insecurities about the situation, and I've learned that continuing to repeat and explain my self in these situations is not going to alleviate my insecurities.

I need to work with and work through my insecurities in my own ways, separate from this necessary boundary setting.

In the present moment, I just need to state my limits with the other person, and then stop talking about it.

SETTING HEALTHY BOUNDARIES

Say Things Cleanly and without Extensive Discussion

This suggestion is a variation of "say things once," and I don't have a lot to say about it.

Saying things cleanly means making "I" statements that are concise and to the point. These statements clearly reflect what you are trying to convey about how you feel and what you want or need. These statements are not muddied by indirect messages, old issues, or accusations.

Saying things without extensive discussion means just what it says. Some discussion may be necessary for effective and fair communication. But beware of extensive discussion. Extensive discussion can easily take us away from our point and away from our center. As we elaborate on our boundaries or as we answer questions and explain our self to the other person, it is easy to lose track of what we were first saying and meaning.

It is easy to slip into the unclear communication that rambles on from one unhappy topic to another. This is especially easy when we are upset and are trying to say things that are difficult for us to say, such as setting boundaries.

We sometimes slip into these tangled moments despite our best efforts, but be assured, we can find our way out.

Take a deep breath and simply return your focus to you. Remind your self of what you wanted to say to the other person, offer it to them in an "I" statement, and leave it at that.

Stick to the Topic

We easily get off the immediate topic when we are upset. In our fury, we pile on this and that, escalating the argument and losing the original point. As we get more and more lost and angry, we pull in more and more old stuff that still makes us mad and causes us pain.

Here is one demonstration, which may seem all-too-familiar, of this getting off the topic:

Chris: "Have you asked off from work yet?"

Blake: "No."

Chris: "When do you plan on asking?"

Blake: "I don't know."

Chris: "What do you mean, 'I don't know'?"

Blake: "Nothing in particular. I don't know."

Chris: "You make me so mad. You never give me a straight answer when I ask you a question."

Blake: "Well you ask too many questions. I'm tired of all your questions. I feel like I'm being cross-examined."

Chris: "Well, somebody needs to cross-examine you. Anybody who'd put off asking for their vacation days needs their head examined. What's wrong with you?"

Blake: "There's nothing wrong with me. You seem to be the one having the problem."

Chris: "I'm not the one with the problem. I'm not the one who put things off and screwed up our vacation last time."

Blake: "Yeah, and I'm not the one who made such a scene in the restaurant that our children refuse to eat out with us anymore."

Chris: "That wouldn't have happened if you had just answered my question then about the checkbook."

Blake: "You and that damn checkbook. You act like the world's going to fall apart if everything isn't just right in it."

Chris: "And you act like you don't care if we have a penny in it. You're terrible with money!"

This argument could go on and on. And it will go on and on if we don't intervene on our own behalf. We get on this angry roll and stuff just keeps coming out of our mouth.

And the original question about the vacation plans is lost. But who wants to go on a vacation at this point, anyway?

Intervening on our own behalf is crucial in this type of situation. We need to be vigilant of our own impulses to insert another issue into the discussion and aware of invitations from the other person to change the subject as well. Often, we are both party to this changing of subjects.

When topics are added on like this, it becomes next to impossible to talk about and resolve *any* of the issues. Instead they are piled up and tangled and, without sorting through them carefully, handling them one by one, we are not able to resolve them. Granted, some topics may be interrelated and need to be considered in this way, but here I am speaking of us loading on topics in angry, accusing ways that avoid dealing with the topic at hand.

We need to be prepared to intervene on our own behalf when the conversation starts to get muddied or when we slip away from the original topic. We need to take note of how we are feeling as we get further into this unproductive argument. We need to be ready to bring our self back to our original question or statement and anchor our self to it—not necessarily stating it again but reminding our self of what is true for us and having that be the foundation for the next thing we say or do. If we are making such efforts to intervene on our own behalf, the above argument may look something like this:

Chris: "Have you asked off from work yet?"

Blake: "No."

Chris: "When do you plan on asking?"

Blake: "I don't know."

Chris: "What do you mean, 'I don't know'?"

Blake: "Nothing in particular. I don't know."

Chris: "You make me so mad. You never give me a straight answer when I ask you a question."

Blake: "Well, you ask too many questions. I'm tired of all your questions. I feel like I'm being cross-examined."

Chris: (*Pausing. Breathing. Listening to self.*) "Okay. I hear you. What I mean to say is that I'm really looking forward to going with you on this trip. In order to get the tickets at the discounted price, I need to make the reservations by Friday."

Blake: "So, why didn't you tell me this before? I never feel like I'm getting clear information from you."

Chris: (*Pausing. Breathing. Listening to self.*) "I'm sure I told you about this deadline when we first talked about the trip. I haven't mentioned it since, because I thought you knew."

Blake: "You make too many assumptions."

Chris: (*Pausing. Breathing. Listening to self.*) "What I am saying now is that I need to know your vacation schedule before Friday in order to get our discounted tickets."

Blake: "There you go with the money stuff again. I don't think these tickets you are getting are at such a good price anyway!"

Chris: (*Pausing. Breathing. Listening to self.*) "Well, I'm calling for my reservations on Friday. If you can go and want me to make your reservations too, let me know. I need to go now."

Again, this is easier said than done. Sticking to the topic can be a real challenge. It can however be useful in untangling our self and whatever is being discussed. By returning to the topic at hand, we can work with that issue until it has a level of clarity or resolution that then frees us to move on to the next, perhaps equally important, topic.

SETTING HEALTHY BOUNDARIES
Stay in the Present

Over the years, many books have been written on the topic of living in the present; in fact, the concept is central to much of Eastern philosophy and religion. Also known as mindfulness, this is the act of being in the present moment. *Full Catastrophe Living* by Jon Kabat-Zinn, and *The Miracle of Mindfulness* by Thich Nhat Hanh, are two such books that offer wonderful details about this practice of mindfulness.

Being in the present moment, or being mindful, can be useful in our efforts to set healthy boundaries with others and with our self. Further on I describe a number of disentangle ideas that employ the wisdom of the above two books and will help you with your cultivation of mindfulness. For now, I simply want to comment on the value of being in the present when we are communicating with someone else and perhaps setting boundaries with them.

It is easy to jump to the future or return to the past when we are entangled. Entanglements have us off-center. We may be worried, upset, confused, or angry. And our mind interacts with our feelings, which creates more turmoil.

Our thoughts rush to catastrophic things that may happen in the future if we stick with our boundaries: The other person may leave me; I will be financially ruined; I will have to be alone; I will never find someone else; and on and on.

Or our thoughts go back to the past, fueling the present fires more than is useful in the present moment: We think of things the person has done, which may not relate to what we are talking about, but that also irritate us; we start to predict their present and future behavior based on how they have responded in the past, failing to allow that perhaps something may be different this time if we are present to it.

So as we interact with the other person about the things we want to get across, our mind may be busy chatting away about these past and future things as well.

These are all obstacles to being in the present moment.

Being in the present moment quiets these thoughts, bringing your focus to the moment-to-moment interactions you are presently having with this person. It means being aware of your body, your thoughts, your feelings, and your actions right now.

It is interesting how many common expressions we use to refer to the decentering of our self that comes from not being in the present. One I have come to appreciate, usually describing anger or upset, is "I was beside my self!" What this means to me is that in that moment, a person is not centered, is not with their self. They feel torn by their emotions, losing touch with their body, mind, and spirit. The person literally feels like they are beside their self and not *with* their self. They are not mindful of what is going on with them at that time.

Another common expression is "I fell to pieces." And, of course, we all know the antidote: "Well, get your self together." Exactly!

A third expression related to this being in the present is "having the presence of mind." A friend helped me to see this expression in action as I related an incident from my day where I had kept my self from creating an angry and unfortunate situation with my daughter.

My daughter and I were supposed to go to a friend's birthday party. I knew I could not pick her up until very close to the time we were expected. I had asked her to be ready, as we would have to leave right away.

I arrived at our house in my hurry-up-let's-go mode, in large part because I was, as usual, running very close to late. As I got out of the car, my daughter greeted me with pleasure. She wanted me to come in and see the gifts and decorations she had created for this friend. She was so tickled with her work.

In that rushing moment, I could have lost it and said, "No! Let's go. I told you to be ready." But, as my friend later pointed out, I had the "presence of mind" to slow my self down, really notice her and her happiness, become aware that I did not want to mess up what she was enjoying, and realize that she was asking for only two minutes of our time.

So I caught my self, joined her in her delight, and we both left for the party calmly and with good feelings.

Being in the present requires that we slow down, get out of our heads, and tune in: tune in to now, to what we are experiencing, and to what is being said to us and happening around us in that moment.

When we are having a heavy-duty conversation or are about to have one, we need to be with our self and remind our self that what is being said is about now and is not a predictor of things to come or an indictment for things past.

In its healthiest form, what is being said now is about now and is best experienced and taken as just that.

SETTING HEALTHY BOUNDARIES
Listen to the Other Person

The suggestion here is to listen to the other person without losing our self to what we are hearing.

The more we are able to listen to the other person and truly and accurately hear what they are saying, the more likely we are to be dealing with reality and not illusions.

And it is of equal importance to be able to listen to them without losing track of what *we* are trying to say, without getting all upset and flying off the handle, or changing our point of view to theirs when we really don't want to.

So how do we do all of this at once? We do it with lots of self-awareness and conscious effort to center and re-center our self as we interact.

The following list offers some specific suggestions to help us with this centered, effective listening:

- Slow down the pace of the conversation.
- Make eye contact with the other person.
- Pay attention to *what* the other person is saying, as well as to *how* they are saying it.
- Notice if *what* is being said matches *how* the person is saying it. Are you hearing one message or are you getting two different messages between the person's verbal and nonverbal communications?
- Seek clarification. Feel free to say, "I don't understand."
- Use "I" statements.
- Inquire as to whether you have heard the person accurately. Tentatively tell them what you think you are hearing from them.
- Don't try to tell the other person what they mean or how they feel.
- Welcome any clarifications if you have heard the other person inaccurately.
- Then repeat back to the person what you now are hearing from them.

The only assignment for our self here is to listen. We are trying to understand what the other person is saying to us. We don't have to do anything more in this moment. We don't have to give them a final answer, make a decision, or conclude anything right now.

As we listen we may have a variety of internal reactions, from surprise and relief, to outright frustration. Whatever we may be experiencing, it is useful to be aware of those feelings and to sit with them for a while, along with what we are hearing from the other person.

Then, as we sort through all this information about our self and the other person, the answers will come.

For the present, just listen.

SETTING HEALTHY BOUNDARIES
Be Careful of Defending, Justifying, and Convincing

As we listen to someone talk to us, we are likely to have emotional reactions to what they are saying. Perhaps we are pleased or excited. We may disagree or even be angered. Or perhaps we are confused, not sure what the other person is trying to say.

If I am confused, I find it useful to say so and to ask for clarification using some of the previous suggestions. Let the person know what you think they are saying, and if they say that is not what they mean and offer more information, again let them know what you hear them say.

When we let the other person know what we are hearing, this helps us to slow down and clarify to our self what they are saying. Often in this type of conflicted conversation, we slip away from our center as we try to get our point across. Repeating out loud what the other person is saying can be very centering for us and helps to ensure that we are working toward communicating and not arguing.

When we are clear about what the other person is saying, it is useful to acknowledge what we are hearing and to stop at that for the present moment.

It is common to defend, rationalize, explain, justify, or convince in reaction to what the other person is saying. It is almost a natural instinct, an attempt to protect our self. My experience, however, is that if I react too quickly in these ways, I can lose my centeredness.

As I react to the situation and to what is being said, I slip into trying to control someone else's reactions and opinions. I want to set things straight. I want to make things right. I become attached to these goals in an unhealthy way and lose track of my original point. And in so doing, I lose track of my self.

I feel off-center. My thoughts become less clear, my behavior more agitated, my tone harsh or insecure, maybe even submissive.

If we are not mindful, we can slip into these reactive behaviors—defending, justifying, and convincing—rather than the conscious actions we want to be taking. Jumping to these reactive behaviors only increases the chances that we will remain entangled, perhaps tightening the web around our self a bit more, leaving us feeling worse than when we began.

We want to be able to respond to what the other person is saying, and if necessary, defend our self in clear and centered ways.

So, go slowly. Listen. Seek clarification. Acknowledge what you hear. Then sit with your self and this information and consciously decide what you want to say or do in response.

SETTING HEALTHY BOUNDARIES
Be Conscious and Observing of Your Self

As we get more deeply involved in an entanglement, we lose touch with our self. We are so caught up in things outside of our self: what the other person is saying or doing, our fears about the future, defending our self in the present, what other people will think.

As we become more and more attached to these things, we lose contact with our self. Not only are we distracted from our original point, we also lose touch with what we are saying and how we are saying it. These are the moments when we say those terrible things we later regret. We are not aware of our tone of voice or our nonverbal behaviors; our actions may become impulsive, without thought or awareness.

We have no "presence of mind."

We are "beside our self," not with our self.

In order to achieve and maintain our centeredness, we must work toward staying with our self.

This means that though we may be very upset, we stay aware of those feelings and develop our ability to actually observe them as we are experiencing them.

This observing is not to be confused with dissociative experiences, where people report being outside their body watching their self. In those experiences, the person usually is feeling unattached to their self. It is like they are observing someone separate from their self and have no power or influence over what is happening.

Here I am speaking of observing the self in a way that is not separate, but rather is consciously taking ownership of who you are, what you are experiencing, and what you are saying and doing.

This conscious observing of your self as you interact with another person means that you are at least as aware of your self as you are of things outside your self.

Usually when we start to lose track of our self, we feel off-center and generally bothered and upset. Sometimes we feel quite lost. In these moments, we want to be aware of how we are feeling and what we are experiencing. This awareness can help us come back to more solid ground.

If I am yelling angrily at someone, I want to simultaneously observe my self doing that. I want to see that "Oh, here I am yelling and saying these things. Is this what I want to be doing? Is this what I want to be saying?" I want to be aware of my tone, my actions, and my physical reactions.

Or, if I am saying "yes" to something when I really want to say "no," I want to be aware that I am doing this and notice what is going on with me as I do. I want to see that "Oh, here I am agreeing to do this when it really is a problem for me. I'm not feeling happy about this. I am even feeling angry that this person has asked me to do this again."

Conscious ownership of our self provides us with an anchor in the storm. It can help us to not make difficult situations even worse; it in fact helps us make difficult situations better for our self. We feel more in control of our self, we convey what we really want to convey, and we thus have fewer regrets and entanglements.

SETTING HEALTHY BOUNDARIES
Learn when to Stop

There is definitely an art to knowing when to stop.

Stopping at the right moment greatly increases the chances of keeping our center and perhaps making our point and generally improves the quality of the communication we are having.

But knowing when to stop can be a challenge. We get on a roll and don't want to stop. We keep repeating our self because "we aren't finished." We keep saying the same thing over and over in a variety of ways, hoping this will help the other person see our point, perhaps even concede. We leave the discussion, then come back to say still more. And even when the other person does concede in some way, we go on and on about why didn't they do this a long time ago, what's wrong with them that they could not see this before, and blah blah blah.

As they say, we "beat it to death." In the process, though, we beat our self and the relationship to death as well. Good spirit goes out the door. Antagonism and defensiveness take over as a matter of course.

So just what is this art of knowing when to stop?

Knowing when to stop involves being with our self during the interaction, and thus becoming aware of when we have said all we need to say for now. It means recognizing signs that we may be starting to lose our center: our increasing defensiveness or efforts to convince, increasing feelings of agitation or irritation, or accusations about topics other than the present one.

Knowing when to stop also involves noticing what is happening outside of our self as well: How is the other person responding?

Are we having a conversation or an argument? Does it feel safe to continue right now?

Knowing when to stop involves being conscious of all of this data in the moment, then intervening on our own behalf.

When we start feeling like we need to stop, that is probably a very good moment to stop. And it can be as simple as saying to your self and to the other person, "I need to stop for right now."

SETTING HEALTHY BOUNDARIES
Stop

The art of stopping is knowing when to stop and then actually stopping.

As with the other ideas for disentangling, this is often easier said than done.

It is hard to stop our self when we are on a roll. It's like trying to stop a sled when you're halfway down the hill and headed for a tree. If you don't stop the sled or get off it in some way, you know what's coming.

So it goes with our discussions with someone else. It may not be a tree, necessarily, perhaps a ditch instead, or some unpleasant obstacle, but that's where we're headed if we continue down this path.

Let's remind our self of the need to stop this roll we are on and avoid the unnecessary consequences of continuing it.

We can save our self and the interaction if we say what we want to say, talk about it with centeredness, tune into when is a good time to stop, and then stop.

Enough said.

SETTING HEALTHY BOUNDARIES
Boundaries and You

Think of someone with whom you want to set a limit or boundary. Perhaps you need to say "no" to something. Perhaps you want to stop doing something you have done in the past. Perhaps you need to stop accepting an unacceptable behavior from someone else. Slow down and take whatever time you need to think about this:

What do you want, need, feel?

What is the boundary you need to set?

What exactly do you want to say to the other person?

What is an "I" statement that will convey your message?

Now think about actually telling the other person about this limit. What are things within you that you need to be aware of in order not to lose your center as you set this limit?

Do you tend to go on and on?

Do you get defensive? Accusatory? Mean?

Do you apologize for having a limit and try to make the other person okay with what you are saying?

Do you tend to bring up unfinished stuff from the past? Or generalize to the future?

What else is true for you?

And now think of tools that could help you to state your limits and not lose your self. What would it be like if you:

First took a deep breath and brought your self fully into the present moment?

Made sure that you paid as much attention to your self in the interaction as to the other person?

Listened to the other person without losing track of you and the point you need to make?

Resisted your impulses to react and took a mental or physical break from the interaction if you were feeling confused, upset, or generally off-center?

Stopped when your good judgment told you to stop?

Now with all of this information, decide what you want to do about setting this boundary and how you are going to do it.

What do you want to say?

What are things about your self you want to be particularly aware of that can lead to further entanglements in this type of situation?

What are tools you are going to try to use to increase the chances of this being a healthy communication that respects you and the other person?

"There's nothing else I can do.
I have to let go."

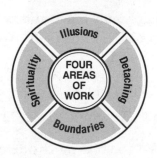

THE FOUR AREAS OF WORK

Developing Spirituality

The process of disentangling would be scary and empty if it did not also involve spiritual growth in our lives. Its presence is vital as we work to apply all of the preceding ideas for disentangling.

Facing illusions, letting go of hopes and ideas to which we have been attached, can be daunting; it requires a grieving process as well as a leap of faith. This leap of faith is the seed of our spirituality. Spirituality stabilizes us. It reminds us that we are not the ultimate power in charge here, that maybe what we think we want is not really what is best for us, and that our letting go of things we cannot control enables things to unfold the way they are meant to.

Detaching from someone or something requires emotional balance and subsequent changes in our behaviors. We often stop doing things for others that we have normally done, and we stop some of the reactive behaviors that have kept our entanglements alive and sick. Making these changes is greatly helped by spirituality. It can be very scary to move away from the other person in these ways. Our feelings of abandonment, guilt, and fear can turn us quickly around, have us doing the same old things, and thus feed the loss of our self in another. Again, spirituality backs us up, supports us, and catches us. Spirituality is our comfort, our place of rest, reassurance, and good company. It is the source of the serenity we seek.

Setting boundaries also implies change. Setting boundaries is about doing things differently than in the past, about us becoming different people by virtue of our setting these limits. Many of us have not previously been good at stating and enforcing what we will and won't accept from others. When we start to do this, everything may start to change. And this is where spirituality comes in. Spirituality offers us help in strengthening the self we are creating. When we are in touch with a power greater than our self, we can better figure out what boundaries are best for us, and gather support as we work to stick with those limits. Spirituality can help us keep our center when we're feeling drawn away from it.

So what do I mean by spirituality?

Spirituality here is personal to you.

In general, I am talking about the concept of a power greater than your self, a concept central to twelve-step programs. This is the belief that we are not the ultimate power in our lives, nor are we in full control of everything. This is not an abdication of responsibility. We certainly need to take responsibility for our self, *and* we need to be able to accept when things are not in our control and turn them over to this greater power.

Specifically, this notion of a greater power is for you to determine. For people with religious beliefs this greater power will most likely be the God of their faith. For some, this greater power may be in nature, in friends, in silence, or in something they love. It could be in any number of things. And for others, spirituality may not be anything particularly tangible or visualized but rather a feeling, an experience that defies easy description. And there are others who find this notion of spirituality so distant, perhaps even foreign, that they have only a glimmer of what this might mean and have little interest or belief in it at all.

Whatever your source of spirituality, however well-developed it may (or may not) be, I have found certain ideas helpful in accessing my higher power and strengthening my spirituality. In so doing, I feel much more centered. Whether I am facing my illusions, detaching, or setting boundaries, spirituality is central to my stability and strength.

The first eight ideas in Developing Spirituality are about "Openings to Spirituality," and are based on mindfulness practices. I've long been a student of Jon Kabat-Zinn's Mindfulness-Based Stress Reduction program (MBSR), which is where I learned about these centering practices. I'm also a student of the twelve-step fellowship for family and friends of alcoholics, and have chosen here to weave together what I've learned from these excellent "schools." The practices that help me to quiet my self and come to the present moment also help me to let go of things I cannot control and access my spiritual life, which is always waiting for me to return to it.

Here are a few of the neurobiological findings from recent research on mindfulness practices. Hopefully, this information will deepen your understanding of how your mind and body are interrelated and will encourage you to apply the ideas of this section, believing in their ability to help you make real and lasting changes in you.

On a basic biological level, mindfulness practices help to oxygenate our body. Anxiety and stress can result in shallow breathing. As we learn to breathe mindfully, our breath naturally drops deeper and we use more of our lung capacity, taking in more oxygen and releasing more carbon dioxide.

From a neuroscience perspective, mindfulness practices help to quiet our limbic system and more effectively employ our neocortex, which facilitates emotional management to reduce reactive behaviors. As we have learned, stress and anxiety are fed by our sympathetic nervous system, which releases adrenaline and cortisol. Mindfulness practices aid the work of the parasympathetic system, which calms and centers us by releasing endorphins and natural opioids.

Research has demonstrated that *changes in brain structure* may underlie some of the improvements reported by people who practice MBSR. People don't just feel better because they are spending time relaxing. Their increase in focus, decreased impulsivity, improved tolerance for negative emotions, and increased feelings of well-being may be attributable to changes in their brains. Through the use of MRI technology, researchers have found *decreased gray-matter density* in the amygdala, known to play an important role in anxiety and stress, and *increased gray-matter density* in the hippocampus, known for learning and memory, as well as other brain structures associated with self-awareness, compassion, and introspection.

The last five ideas in Developing Spirituality are about "Beyond the Openings to Spirituality." Once you have quieted your self and come to the present moment with awareness of both internal and external sensations, contact with a power greater than your self—if you choose to incorporate this belief into your life—becomes deeper, richer, and more meaningful.

DEVELOPING SPIRITUALITY
Slow Down

We go so fast in our lives. Our hours and days are filled with things we want to do, have to do, or think we have to do. A client once said to me, "I'm living my life off of a list."

How easily we have slipped into this fast pace, this high level of activity! We live in a world full of data and opportunities, one that has many of us filling many roles at once: parent, breadwinner, caregiver of aging parents, housekeeper, mechanic, gardener, homemaker, chief cook, and bottle washer. We can barely get done in a day what we think needs to get done. And often we don't.

As we speed up, moving mindlessly from one activity to the next, our spirituality does not even occur to us; our mind is too busy thinking of what we are going to do next. I know I am guilty of this. After many years of this behavior, I caught my self red-handed. I finally noticed when, after working hard to put a good meal on the table and gather the family all together, the first phrase out of my mouth once everyone had food on their plate was "After this let's . . ."

"After this let's . . ." What a great way not to slow down and enjoy the fruits of my efforts and the gifts of the present: good food, family time , silence, relaxation, who knows what else.

"After this let's . . ." What a great way to keep moving and not stop. Without a doubt, that's what I was doing. I was feeling the need to keep moving. Things to do, plans to be made.

But I now realize those things will happen anyway. So why not slow down for the moment and be there?

Several days each week, I start my work-away-from-home day later in the morning. On these mornings, I walk our daughter to school out here in the country. Then I go on my own walk. I walk for exercise and for meditation. I consider my self lucky to be able to walk at this time of day. The day is fresh and delightful. And at some point during the walk, I will stop completely, and stand very still.

Stopped there, I become increasingly aware of this earth upon which I stand. I notice the sounds of the birds and the breeze and the river. I see the Blue Ridge Mountains before me; I notice the rocks and colors there. I am aware of the steadiness and peacefulness of it all. And I am struck by the fact that all this will remain the haven it is, while I run out into the world doing my thing. The creek beside our house will keep flowing over the rocks with its refreshing sounds; the sun will track its familiar course, warming our home and creating gorgeous lighting as the day nears its end.

Standing still helps me to see all this, and to feel the serenity and stability that come by bringing all of this into my awareness. Without my efforts to slow down and even stop, there is a good chance I would miss all of this wonder.

DEVELOPING SPIRITUALITY
Simplify

Some mornings, I can hardly write because of the lists in my mind. Today I went on my morning walk, and my mind chattered on about things I could do with the hour I have before my daughter and I head off to church. It is an unreasonable list, intrusive and persistent, and each of the items on it beckons.

The list goes something like this: work on the book, finish sewing two pillows for the front porch chairs, call my brother and invite him to supper, call my friend about our canoeing plans this afternoon, take a shower, get breakfast for us, get dressed, and go.

I chuckle now as I write this list. I know it is ridiculous; seeing it on paper and telling you about it only emphasizes its absurdity.

What I have to do is simplify. I have to do this over and over in a day. Obviously, I cannot check off each list item in the one hour I have before church. In fact, I probably couldn't get it done by the end of the day. It's just too much.

So I listen to my self and allow things on the list to call to me as they will and then choose consciously how I want to spend my precious time. Today I have chosen writing over sewing. In my sicker days, I would've tried to do both. This morning I am well enough to know better.

Simplifying is about weeding out some of the extras, so what we choose to keep can grow and flourish, not be choked out by rushing, anxiety, and frustration.

Simplifying is about editing our lists, so what we choose to keep will be clear and strong, and we will feel clear and strong.

When we are not choked out by rushing, anxiety, and frustration, when we feel clear and strong, we can better access our spirituality. We can take a breath, be with our self and what we are doing, and make contact with our higher power.

As I walked this morning, practicing letting these thoughts about my list go, I suddenly came upon two rabbits stopped in their tracks. I stopped, too. And the three of us stood watching each other for ever so long. I took time to notice their coats and eyes and tails. They did not seem afraid, though they stood still as statues. We were all just standing still on this earth, letting go of our lists for the day and being with each other and our self. A squirrel then crossed the road to join us, but only briefly, as its activity sent the rabbits running off in two directions, the squirrel up a tree, and me on down the road.

But we all stopped and met each other this morning. We simplified life, even if it was just for those passing moments. It was delightful and refreshing, and a good reminder of what I speak about.

I need to simplify in many aspects of my life, from lists, to possessions, to thoughts. We clutter our lives with stuff and mental chatter. In so doing, we miss the great moments right before our eyes and hearts.

DEVELOPING SPIRITUALITY
Be in the Present

Back in my high school days I was a cheerleader. At times when I think about being in the present, I remember a cheer we used to rally the crowds with:

> *Lean to the Left.*
> *Lean to the Right.*
> *Stand Up.*
> *Sit Down.*
> *Fight! Fight! Fight!*

Now why would this cheer come to mind in this context? My guess is it reminds me of the way some of my days go:

> *Rally Here.*
> *Rally There.*
> *Run-a-Round*
> *And*
> *Do! Do! Do!*

This is a chant that stirs me, moving me away from the moment, into thoughts and action. A more accurate version might be:

Look to the Past.

Look Ahead.

Worry.

Fret.

We're as Good as Dead!

Dead? Yes, dead. If I'm into my thoughts, plans, actions, and schedules, I'm very likely missing the moment I am in, and it is as though I was never there.

How many times have we wondered if we turned off a burner or turned down the wood stove? We weren't there. How many times do we not remember something someone said to us? We weren't there.

Over and over through the course of a day we leave the present moment. In fact, I have to make a conscious effort to be in the present, reminding my self to hear, see, feel, smell, and experience what is happening right now.

By bringing my self to the present moment, I discover such richness there, richness in senses and emotions. And I believe that richness is a tap to deeper spirituality.

Bringing my self to the present moment greatly increases the chances that I can access my spirituality.

When I am in my head and in action, I can easily forget the bigger picture. I can forget that there is anyone other than me to see that all of this gets done, that there is a wonderful world right here and now and a power greater than me at work in it.

Being in the present moment brings me back to life and spirit.

DEVELOPING SPIRITUALITY
Find Some Solitude

I have had some resistance to putting to paper my thoughts on finding solitude.

Perhaps it's because I have some resistance in my self to finding solitude. I stay busy and move from one thing to another, often with no break in between. Some part of me just hates to stop what I'm doing until I finish. And I am never finished.

Being a mother, a wife, a daughter, a sister, a friend, and a breadwinner, I have literally no time for solitude from others unless I make sure it happens for me.

Solitude is about time for my self to be with my self. Solitude is about minimizing external distractions and interruptions for a while.

We think of solitude as being out in nature, on a quiet walk in the woods or along the shore. Or we imagine a retreat in some remote area, some sanctuary or meditation space. Yes, each of these places can be a wonderful source of solitude.

Practically speaking, however, these types of places for solitude are not necessarily accessible to us on a daily basis. This is no reason not to find solitude in ways that *can* work for us.

I have a space for my self in my bedroom, where I have my books, some possessions from childhood, and a comfortable place to sit or lie down. I also have a couple of places on our property that are good for solitude.

I imagine you are aware of such spaces in your own world, or if not, I would suggest they are there waiting to be found.

Sometimes solitude comes simply by closing the door, not answering the phone, and turning off the television, radio, and computer.

Solitude can be had by setting boundaries with others and prioritizing our self. Getting to this solitude rarely just happens. We have to make it happen. It is a self-imposed time-out.

We have to tell our children, our partner, our parents, our siblings, our friends, our coworkers, and clients, that we will "get back with them" but we first need to take a break. We need to tell our self this is okay to do, that it is okay to temporarily let go of our roles and responsibilities in order to restore our self and our spirit.

We don't have to spend a long time in solitude to gain some benefits. Granted, an entire day would be great. But let's not wait around for *that* to happen.

A departure into thirty minutes of solitude can make a noticeable difference for me when I need to re-center my self. An hour is fabulous. You can learn what works for you. The point here is that some time in solitude is better than none.

Let's not wait around for the right place and the right time for solitude. The opportunity is not likely to just happen. And without solitude, we get sicker, madder, and more anxious and stressed.

Solitude helps us get back in touch with our physical and emotional self. We become quieter, calmer, and more centered. Our awareness increases, and our mind clears. We open our self more to the broader picture of life and the presence of powers greater than our self in and with us.

DEVELOPING SPIRITUALITY
Breathe

Bring your focus to your breath.

This is not a new idea. Following the breath has always been a cornerstone of meditation and mindfulness. Wonderful and extensive books have been written on the topic and provide excellent guidelines to using the breath. Thich Nhat Hanh's *The Miracle of Mindfulness* and Jon Kabat-Zinn's *Wherever You Go, There You Are* are two good examples.

For the purposes of this book, I will simply address the importance of bringing focus back to our breath as a means of calming our self and returning to our self. For some this is a reminder. For others, this notion may be relatively new.

As we get unhealthily attached and entangled, we get further and further away from our self. Such attachments can simply be about trying to get everything done on our "To-Do" list for the day or trying to get our children or partners to do something we think they should do.

With entanglements, our focus strays more and more to things outside our self; at our worst we are essentially disconnected from our mind, body, heart, and spirit.

Bringing our focus to our breath brings us back to our self. Rather than doing one thing and thinking about another, we are bringing our physical and mental selves into accord. Rather than being riveted by the external, we regain contact with the internal.

Focusing on your breath is a simple and powerful way to almost immediately reconnect with you, which is the heart of the path out of entanglements.

Focusing on your breath means just that: bring your awareness to your inhalations and exhalations.

- As you inhale, notice the feeling of the air through your nose.
- Notice your chest rise.
- Notice the moment when you slightly pause between the inhalation and exhalation.
- As you exhale, notice your chest fall.
- Notice muscles in your body letting go.
- Repeat this slowly for a while. As you do so, you may find that your breaths are deepening, that you inhale longer and have longer sustained exhales.
- As thoughts come to your mind, simply bring your focus back to your breath, over and over.

We can focus on our breath anywhere, anytime. Certainly, it is a wonderful way to reconnect with our self when we have some solitude. But again, let's not wait for only those special times.

We can renew our self even in the middle of an argument or a worry, if we bring our focus to our breath. When we start feeling driven, anxious, overloaded, or agitated, focusing on our breath can help us to re-center and relax.

I think of following and deepening my breath as a way to reset my internal thermostat. As my breathing deepens, I feel my blood pressure go down, my muscles relax, and my body temperature drop. I am no longer as attached to all the things I felt were so important. I am back in touch with my self. I feel calmer, safer, and better able to access my spirituality.

DEVELOPING SPIRITUALITY
Relax Your Body

The amount of tension we carry around in our body is actually quite remarkable. We carry it in our neck, shoulders, and back. We grind our teeth, tighten our jaw. We clench our fists, knot our stomach. We keep a perpetual smile or frown. Our muscles are tight and rigid.

Sometimes we are aware of this tension. Often we are not.

Entanglements invite us to neglect our physical self. We lose sleep, skip meals, or overeat for comfort. We overextend our bodies to accommodate others, and put off routine care, including medical and dental appointments, for our self.

Often we are so out of touch with our self that we are not aware of this tightness in our body until it starts to scream at us in the form of chronic pain or illness.

Making contact with our physical self is essential to disentangling. In fact, contact with our physical self can be an access to other parts of our self, including emotional feelings and spirit.

In *Full Catastrophe Living*, Jon Kabat-Zinn recommends the body scan as a means of tuning in to the body. With a quiet mind, lie or sit in a comfortable posture. Then progressively move your focus through your entire body from head to toe, or vice versa, noticing any sensations you may have in each body part. In your mind's eye, breathe in and out through that body part. For example:

- Starting with your feet, bring your focus to that part of your body.
- Notice any sensations you may have in your feet.
- Notice them making contact with whatever surface they're on.

- Notice the feeling of your shoes or socks or the air touching them.

- Really pay attention to your feet: What do you notice?

- Using your mind's eye, follow your breath as it flows in and out of your feet.

- And now notice your calves . . .

Once we are in touch with our body, we can respond to its needs. Relaxation is one of those needs. Many people I counsel describe their problems as related to high levels of stress. And my experience is that when I am entangled with someone else, my stress level is chronically high.

So, relax.

Well, how?

People have lots of relaxation ideas that work for them:

- Hot showers.

- Hot tubs.

- Long walks.

- Yoga.

- Reading.

- Meditation.

- Deep breathing.

- Massage.

- Time with pets.

- Time with friends.

- Time alone.

- Listening to music.

- Making music.
- Writing.
- Coloring.
- Artwork.
- Mindless television.

Get to know your body, paying particular attention to where you put your tension. Most of us have at least a couple places we routinely tighten and hold. Find yours, and notice the body's sensations there. Then respond by breathing in and out through that part of your body to help you let go and relax.

Become aware of what helps you relax your body, and try to do it often.

Relaxing the body brings us back to our self. It calms us, re-centers us, and opens the path to our heart and spirit.

DEVELOPING SPIRITUALITY
Quiet Your Mind

Entanglements are not about quiet minds. When we are entangled with someone else, our mind chatters on and on about them. Whether we are with that person or not, we think about what they are doing. We think about what we said to them, what we wish we had said to them, what we regret saying to them. We think about how they may feel about us, about what they said or may say to us. And on and on.

We are preoccupied.

Our mind gets worn out.

And we are bound to lose our self.

Our mind is so busy with all these thoughts about the past and the future and external things, that we are not paying any attention to our self.

Quieting our mind is central to disentangling. We need to become aware of the busyness of our thinking, and learn to manage it. We need to notice these obsessive thoughts, and intervene on our own behalf. We cannot begin to disentangle until we learn to quiet this thinking of ours.

Many of us find this difficult. Some find it almost impossible. I believe that with conscious effort and practice, it can be done. Quieting the mind means having the ability to dismiss thoughts. We can consciously choose whether to think about something or not. We can say to our self, "I'll think about that later," or "I'm going to stop thinking about that because I can't do anything about that now."

We can quiet our mind by repeatedly bringing our self back into the present.

Bringing our focus to our breath can instantly bring us out of our head and into the moment.

Reminders to our self that we are worrying about things way too far ahead or too far in the past, can bring us back to the here and now. Reminders to our self that we are thinking about things over which we have no control can be useful in letting go and resting our mind.

To quiet the mind, we need to first get in touch with its chatter. This shouldn't be that hard.

Then we need to make the decision to let go of these thoughts. We need to have had enough of them and to desire to be free of them.

And then we need to find a way of quieting the mind that works for us. Many of the ideas previously described can help with this:

- Slow down.
- Simplify.
- Be in the present.
- Find some solitude.
- Breathe.
- Relax your body.

We need to be kind to our self as we work on quieting our mind. It is normal for our heads to be full of thoughts, so don't criticize your self for the way your thoughts jump back in there. Don't give up on learning how to quiet them. It takes practice, but you can do it.

And the benefits are tremendous: A break from the old mental tapes that have played and played in your head. A clear head. An empty, resting mind. Some peace. And you may well find you want to make some changes in those old mental tapes.

DEVELOPING SPIRITUALITY
Sit in Silence

On a daily basis our minds are full of thoughts, and we have lists of lists. We rush from one activity to the next, and while busy with one we are thinking about the other: "When we finish this, let's . . ."

And when we are entangled, our minds and our days can be even busier. Not only do we have our own lists in mind, we have lists for others—lists of what they should do, what they haven't done, what we wish they would do. We have imaginary thoughts about others that go on and on. Some are fun; some disturb us.

All of this fills our mind and our time.

The notion of stopping all this for a while and sitting in silence is a healthy one, but some of us do not naturally gravitate to it. We get so caught up in our thoughts and lists, we rush without awareness from one thing to another. We are reluctant to stop, for even a brief while, to be quiet. We are so afraid we won't get done what needs to be done that we "just can't stop."

And some of us just don't like to be in a stopped, silent place. It is too uncomfortable, unfamiliar, scary even.

Rather than being "a waste of time" or "another thing on our list," sitting in silence can be a refueling of our self. Sitting in silence can help us stop this thinking and doing *ad nauseam*, and see things more clearly, with improved perspective. It can help us to reconnect with our self.

A dear friend of mine suggested that we pause for several minutes between each of our daily activities, and do nothing.

To that idea I would add the suggestion that in those breaks we turn off the television, radio, or music, put aside our reading materials, and decline conversations in the room, on the phone, or on the computer. This is not a time to do that "little extra something."

This is a time to do nothing and to be silent.

We find numerous opportunities for this in our day as we become aware of them. I have noticed one such moment, which I call the "Microwave Moment."

One evening at work, I popped my meal into the microwave for four minutes. I *immediately* thought, "Now what can I do for four minutes? A phone call? Some copying?" Then I caught my self in this using-every-minute mode, this nonstop rushing from one thing to another. I told my self, "No. Just sit still. How about doing nothing for four minutes? How about just being silent and present in this quiet moment?" And so, I had my Microwave Moment.

Silence can be restful. Silence can be our friend. It can be scary, too, if we are afraid of what may come up for us without our busyness to defend our self.

But defending our self through busyness is not really protecting our self so much as losing our self. Our busyness takes us away from our thoughts, feelings, and general awareness. It invites us to lose our self in whatever else we are doing or thinking. It invites us to lose our self in other people and other things.

A break into silence is a direct invitation to come back to our self, to listen to nothing other than our breathing, and to notice, only notice, the physical and emotional sensations present in and with us.

I am sure there are daily opportunities for you to indulge in this silence, if only for moments. I invite you to become aware of them and practice sitting with them for your self.

DEVELOPING SPIRITUALITY
Discover Your Higher Power

All I have to do to accept the idea of a power greater than my self is to look at the world around me.

Just this morning, my husband, daughter, and I walked a trail in a Vermont state park. Gorgeous ferns proliferated on the ground and on rocks. Numerous brooks ran down the side of the hill, creating pools among moss-covered rocks. Silver maples and birch trees reached high into the sky. The loons cried out from the lake below. The balance and cycles of the natural world surrounded and filled us.

A power greater than my self was at work here.

We look at our children, at flowers, at vegetables, at animal life, and know there is a power greater than our self.

In less immediately tangible ways as well, we can come to know a power greater than our self. Our higher power can offer us wisdom, strength, guidance, comfort, and protection beyond what we can do or imagine.

Those of us prone to entanglements sometimes act as if we are fully in charge, fully responsible for everything. The concept of a power greater than our self comes neither to our mind (because it is so cluttered), nor to our spirit (because we are so out of touch with it).

Of immense benefit to disentangling is the discovery of your higher power. We can save our self by not relying completely on our own personal resources. We can and do exhaust them, only to find those resources alone cannot get us out of our entanglements to the happiness we seek.

Entanglements arise from our deeply held belief that we know what is best for us and others, and we pursue those ends with a vengeance, convinced we know how to achieve them.

We get into deep trouble with our self when we cannot allow that perhaps we may not know what is best for us or others, and that a power greater than our self is with us and supporting us. There is a higher power to whom or to which we can let go of things that are beyond our control.

Discovering your higher power is up to you. This is a personal decision and relationship. Those of you who have a God you know and rely on through your religious beliefs probably have this God as your higher power. Those of you who do not subscribe to a particular religious faith may discover your higher power in any form you wish: man, woman, spirit, animal, within you, within a group, in nature—to name just a few.

Discovering your higher power means you decide that you are not the whole show, that there is something beyond your self with which you would like to make a connection.

Your task is to slow your self down, quiet your pushing and pulling, and set out to hear, feel, and experience the constant presence of your higher power.

DEVELOPING SPIRITUALITY
Have an Ongoing Relationship with Your Higher Power

Awakening to the higher power in your life is not just about calling upon that power once a day, occasionally, or when trouble appears.

The spirituality that heals calls for a constant, ongoing relationship with your higher power. Your contact with that power can be made moment by moment in ways both personal and comforting: prayer, meditation, conversations, walks, silence, breathing, and so on.

In order to develop a relationship, I need to spend time with my higher power, listening to that power and trusting it. I can do these things in a silent wood, in the middle of a meeting, or during an argument at home. I often make sure I'm in touch with my higher power as I enter what I anticipate will be a difficult situation. I am in touch with my higher power when I feel good and grateful.

Entanglements are essentially the opposite of spirituality and contact with our higher power. Entanglements strip us of our spirit. Without knowing it, we are selling our soul—and all the rest of our self, too—to someone else, in the hope that this will create the relationship we seek. It is not even that they are asking this of us. We just decide, consciously or not, that such giving of our self will produce the end we desire.

But it doesn't. Instead we find our self tense and anxious, frequently trying to manipulate and control people and situations, even in ways that may seem useful and kind. We feel empty and alone.

We need not give our souls to anyone. Disentangling is about seeing how we've been doing this and working on stopping it. Cultivating an ongoing relationship with your higher power is of great value in ending this soul giveaway.

A relationship with your higher power will strengthen your ability to cultivate a healthy relationship with someone else.

When we have a healthy, ongoing relationship with our higher power, we can learn when to let go of things beyond our control, and we have backup support with us as we let go of things to which we have clung so tightly. We have comfort when we are afraid, company when we are confused, and support when we need to act. We don't have to seek these thing so adamantly and exclusively from others. They are in and with us all the time.

Yes, you will lose contact with your higher power over the course of a day. I certainly do. All of a sudden I catch my self trying to force some solution, trying to make something happen, becoming too attached to doing or getting something. I back off by reconnecting with my higher power. I do this over and over: entangle, then let go.

So, don't be discouraged when you find your self out there again, ripping and tearing, trying to make everything happen on your own.

With an ongoing relationship with your higher power, all you have to do is become aware when you have lost contact and are trying to control things over which you have no control—then, simply, to reconnect. The relief that follows can be great.

DEVELOPING SPIRITUALITY
Let Go of Things You Cannot Control

Several years ago, I was explaining disentangling to an interested person to whom this was a relatively novel idea. One of the things I mentioned was that disentangling entails "letting go."

"Letting go of what?" they asked.

I paused briefly to think it over, not wanting the concept of disentangling to come across as passive or as giving up or giving in.

"Disentangling is about learning to let go of things we have no control over," I responded.

"Oh," they said, with a hint of informed reflection.

Many of our entanglements come from trying to control things over which we have no control. And often we don't have a clue we're doing this. We think what we are doing for the other person is kind, helpful, logical, natural, and desirable. We get so caught up in our own notions about how things are or how we want them to be, that we are not in touch with whether we can or cannot do something about them.

We act as though we can do something about everything. But we can't.

Knowing the difference between what we can and cannot control is essential to disentangling. It can be a challenge sometimes. Without awareness, we jump right in to make something happen or to fix something, and there we are, entangled again.

Some things we can control, and some we cannot.

We can control:

- Where we are.
- Whom we are with.
- What we think.
- What we do with our money, time, or possessions.
- How we handle our feelings.

We cannot control:

- Where other people go.
- Whom they are with.
- What they think.
- What they do with their money, time, or possessions.
- How they handle their feelings.

A point of clarification here: We are learning to identify what we cannot control, and how to let go of trying to control it. This is so we don't keep beating our head against the wall and burning up good time, energy, and spirit.

This does not mean, however, that you have to put up with unacceptable behaviors from someone else.

You may identify some things that you cannot control and can let them go. For example,

> You have been wanting a friend to apply for a job you believe is perfect for them, but they haven't made even one call about it. You've talked to your friend at least three times about this, with no real interested response from them.

> It's probably time to let go.

You may identify other things that you cannot control *and* that you cannot live with. For example,

> Your partner is frequently critical of you. They insult your efforts and discourage you in the things you enjoy. They call you derogatory names and make fun of you in front of others. You have repeatedly told them to stop this behavior, but they haven't stopped.

> You can't make them stop, but you don't have to live with it either. This is where boundaries come in. You can tell your self and them that you won't do _____ if they continue to do these things.

In either case, the process of letting go can be helped by our spirituality.

Spirituality reminds us of the bigger picture, which we often cannot see for the picture we are creating in our mind. Spirituality provides the arena into which we let things go that we cannot control, relinquishing responsibility with trust and faith—not faith that things will happen as we want them to, but faith that life will unfold as it will, and that we can learn to live with what is.

DEVELOPING SPIRITUALITY
Practice These Things

One of the basic concepts of disentangling is that it is a process that takes time. It takes a while for us to make the cognitive, emotional, behavioral, and spiritual changes I speak of. One thing you can do to help with these changes is to practice these ideas.

By practice, I mean at least two things.

On the one hand, practice means to try some or all of these ideas in the spirit of learning—how to perform them, and how to improve in your performance. This is like practicing piano lessons or basketball shots. Only by bringing our self to the situation with awareness and focus, then taking the risks inherent to learning something new, will we be able to disentangle with skill and serenity.

On the other hand, practice means to bring these "Ideas for Disentangling" into your daily life. Make them a part of your way of life. Don't save them for emergencies, treating them like ammunition from a stockade, to be grappled for in moments of desperation. Weapons can be dangerous if we are not practiced in their use; the "Ideas for Disentangling" can backfire on us if we haven't worked to incorporate them into our lives with deep understanding and a healthier self.

Daily practice of spirituality is especially important. Practicing our spirituality can calm us, re-center us, and clear our brain. Spirituality can provide an anchor in the storms we encounter. But again, in order to know where that anchor is and how to use it effectively, we need to have it in our daily practice.

I say daily, but I don't really mean just once a day. My experience is that I am in contact with my higher power many times over the course of the day. When things are good, when things are bad, when there's nothing much happening at all—all are opportunities for me to practice my spirituality.

How do you practice? What does practice mean? Again, that's personal to you. I've suggested many ideas to help you access your spirituality: slow down, relax the body, quiet the mind, breathe, etc. The same way that each of us gets to know our own higher power, we can each develop our own practice to access that power and reap the benefits of our relationship to it.

So, figure out what the practice of *your* spirituality looks like. Maybe you already know, and follow your practice. Keep it up. If all this is new to you, try different avenues for contact with your self and your higher power, and see what feels good to you. Then practice those ways of contact.

Practice means that we are weaving spirituality into our lives. Just as threads woven together can create a beautiful fabric, weaving a daily practice of spirituality into our lives can help to create a lovely and strong self.

DEVELOPING SPIRITUALITY
Cultivate Faith

When I first started my work on disentangling, I remember feeling lonely. I was doing the things I understood would help me get the emotional balance and centeredness I needed, but in the process I felt disconnected and alone, skeptical about what I was doing, and fearful that all I would get out of the process was empty distance.

I talked about this to some friends who were ahead of me on this path. They understood what I was talking about; they'd been there as well. Each of them assured me that as they continued to grow and develop their healthy self, they felt less and less lonely.

I told my self that if I had faith, I too would eventually feel more comfortable with my new relationship with my self and others and not experience it as loneliness. I told my self to just keep practicing my new ways, with the faith that they would help me to feel more serene and content with my self, by my self.

At a later station of my journey, I was speaking with one of my mentors about making a big change in my life. I remember seeing this potential change as a great risk; I did not know what would happen if I made the change. I had no idea how others would react to it or what they might do. I had no idea what I would do or how I would feel. All of these unknowns frightened me a great deal and, for years, had kept me from taking some action.

My mentor's response to all of this was to warmly and gently remind me that to make these changes required "a leap of faith" on my part.

The controlling, exacting part of me wants to know precisely what will happen when changes occur: If _____, then _____. But life doesn't work this way. Often we have to make a decision or a change that we've calculated to be in our best interest, without having any idea what the fallout will be.

This is where faith is everything.

Faith creates a bridge for us from the known to the unknown, from who we are today to who we may become. Faith enables us to move on things that have had us stuck. Faith enables us to do things we didn't think we could do, to continue when we didn't think we could.

And what is this faith in? As with the other areas of spirituality and higher power, faith is to be designed by you. For me, faith is my belief that there is a bigger picture out there, bigger than the one I'm seeing and managing, and I need to do my part *and* allow that bigger picture to unfold as well. It is the taking of responsibility within my limits while allowing life to simultaneously unfold, being present and aware and responding as is healthy for me.

My faith is my trust in the process of living this way. My faith is in an ongoing relationship with my higher power that helps me to believe that I am okay and that what I need will be or actually is here already.

Faith comes with time. It is a deeper aspect of spirituality that we come to know as we travel on our path, making scary changes and feeling alone. Faith is the light in our dark times and an ever-present source of comfort and strength.

I rarely feel lonely anymore.

DEVELOPING SPIRITUALITY
Spirituality and You

**Take a moment to consider spirituality
in your present life:**

Is spirituality present?

Is it important to you?

Does it make a difference in your life?

Do you see any value in it?

Would you like to make any changes
in your spirituality?

**If you find your self wanting to make
spirituality more a part of your life, please
read on.**

**Consider what you already do in your life
that cultivates your spirituality, and jot down
some of those ideas.**

How do you make contact with your
spirituality?

How often do you access your spirituality,
and under what circumstances?

**Now review the list of ideas in this past
section on spirituality. Maybe you can simply
look at the list in the Table of Contents to give
your self an overview of the ideas.**

Which of the ideas naturally appeal to you
most at this time?

Which of the ideas interest you as something you
would like to add to your life?

Which of the ideas can be realistically added
to your current life situation?

**Considering all of these ideas, what are
present paths you wish to develop in order
to cultivate your spirituality?**

What do you want to keep doing?

What do you want to add as ways to
develop your spirituality?

What are obstacles to your doing these things?

What can you do to resolve these obstacles?

*Imagine what your life might be like
with greater spirituality.*

"Life is too short to be hurt by others."

"I'm starting to think: 'What do I want?'"

"I never realized this thirst for new things."

"Breath of fresh air is in my head."

WHEN YOU'VE FOUND YOUR SELF

"Disentangling helps me to feel free
and loving at the same time."

"I am growing."

"I have a new layer of health."

"I feel happier and more hopeful."

"I feel renewed and invigorated
to continue on my path."

"Life-changing stuff."

"When I think about what I've learned, I think I've made great strides."

7 YOUR HEALTHY SELF

*"There's nothing more important to me than my serenity.
That's what motivates me the most to disentangle. I've
learned that the serenity I lose by trying to make my point
or have things my way is not worth it. I have come to know
what serenity feels like, and that's what I want for me."*

Nancy at age forty-eight

Life can be pretty amazing. I turn sixty-seven next week. I will
begin the next twenty-or-so years of my life. This is interesting
timing to me. This book has evolved in blocks of twenty-or-so
years.

I am grateful to be alive to enter my fourth twenty-or-so years, and
I will certainly be living this material, which is dear to my heart
and has made a great difference in my life and my relationships. I
have a healthier self as a result of all I have learned and practice.
I am not always in balance with my self, but I notice when I am
not, and I know how to respond kindly to my self to restore that

precious balance I seek—balance within, and balance with others and with the activities of my life.

Applications of the Four Areas of Disentangle Work

I believe it is useful to have a picture of what we are working toward and what recovery looks like. It is easy to know what we are tired of, don't like, and don't want; it is crucial to know what we do like and do want for our self.

To richly color this picture of our found self, I now bring in the voices of people who have been on this path and have shared their progress with me over many years. I've known these people through counseling, workshops, weekend retreats, and twelve-step fellowships. They are of varied ages and walks of life. These are people who appreciated what they were learning and chose to not only read this material, but also work toward applying it in their life on a daily basis:

> *"I am grateful for all that you're able to communicate so clearly about the disease of codependence . . . what it is— so that we can recognize it—and how we can grow into healthier and happier people on this earth."*

> *"I liked trying to find a path for me with concrete motion— simplifying my thoughts, charts, and fill-in-the-blank—it is hard for me to see the forest for the trees . . . I probed deeper than I expected and feel as if it is the only helpful path."*

> *"Thank you for sharing and for making these ideas accessible and workable."*

Blending their voices with mine, here are some ways we are using the four areas of disentangling to find, develop, and cherish our self, remembering they are not meant to be addressed in any particular order. They are not a checklist. Rather, we may be using skills in one area and realize we would do well to add skills from another area to increase our clarity, centeredness, and effectiveness.

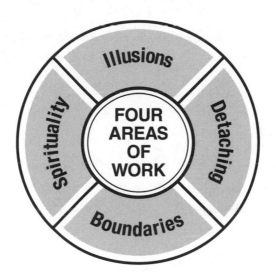

On **Facing Illusions**

"I was grieving for what I thought was."

"I thought I had to live with it, but I don't."

I am careful to notice if I am falling prey to some **Illusion**. Am I not seeing the reality of something? Of someone? Of my self? Am I carrying hope too far? Am I expecting things to be different and still getting the same results? Can I live with the reality I find? If I keep getting mad or sad about something, have I slipped back into believing something that isn't real? These are important questions. I want to see things as they are in real time and not fool my self. This level of honesty can be quite sobering, grim, even disappointing at times. And I know it can be freeing. I have felt that freedom, and I like it.

"The person I was married to only exists in my mind."

"The whole marriage was a lie."

"I do realize I let things decide how I'm going to feel."

"I'm feeling uneasy about the way I used to feel. I wasn't clear-headed. It felt like he drugged me."

"My eyes are clear."

On **Detaching**

"I think that my work is helping me be aware of myself more and what some of my sometimes thoughtless default paths have been and are . . . I do hope I can continue to operate from this more thoughtful space."

"I can't make him better."

"I thought I could turn her around."

I **Detach** whenever it is necessary, whenever I am aware that I could fall into reacting rather than conscious acting. I don't get this perfect every time. Sometimes I just react to something said or done. Immediately afterward, I am aware that my serenity is gone, and I don't like that feeling. So, I try to pause, breathe, and listen before I respond.

An extension of the line-down-the-page exercise, presented in "Entanglements and You," is infinitely useful to me. I am a visual person, meaning I prefer to have at least some mental picture to help me understand something. The line-down-the-page helps with this. I imagine a line between my self and the other person. It is a vertical line, drawn through space, that separates us. The line is not a wall, simply a demarcation of where I end and the other person begins. We are, in fact, different people. With this in mind, when I interact with the person on the other side of the line, I know to go only to the line, and leave my suggestion, offer, or request there. The other person then has the space and freedom to come to the line, examine what I have put there, and respond for their self. Any efforts I make to push my agenda across the line or pull the other person across the line onto my side, leave me at increased risk of losing my self. I have come a long way in learning to stay on my side of the line and not press this boundary.

> "I have a more accurate concept of my whole self and the important purpose of my false self, which up to now I have rejected."

> "It's a free world out there. You don't let your family rule who you see."

> "I've not done anything wrong."

> "I didn't care if I didn't have nothing."

> "She's always in the back of my mind . . . I can't help her . . . I wish I could . . . I wish she'd admit to her problems . . . I can't let that bother me."

> "I'm working on letting go of his stuff. I'm not going to let this bother me."

> "I wonder if I am in touch with myself enough to know what my needs are and to allow others (very capable people) to take care of their own problems."

On Setting Healthy Boundaries

> "I've changed: I'm saying exactly what I feel."

"I wanted to call and tell him, but it would have riled me up more."

"I'm tired of being the giver all the time."

I work on **Boundaries** all the time: boundaries with time, boundaries with people, boundaries with ideas and plans for the day, boundaries with what I can and cannot accept from others, boundaries with self. I am a handful for me to manage—full of ideas, hopes, dreams, conversations, and inspirations. I will never in this lifetime be able to do all the things I want to do; I'm not discouraged by this at all. It makes me more aware of the importance of paying attention to the choices I make about how to use the time I have.

The weekend retreats I offer twice a year are called Codependence Camp. My colleague and I have facilitated twenty-seven of these camps over the past sixteen years. Our topics for camp workshops vary each time. For several, we have worked on boundaries. One of these utilized creative arts to help our self define our boundaries. Working with felt, I made a small banner on which I created a collage from magazine pictures and words to represent what I want my life to look like: Good Marriage, Good Deals, Comfortable Home, Traveling Expeditions, and Relaxation.

Interspersed in this collage were the numerals 1, 5, 6, and 8. Each has a meaning to me: I want to get eight hours of sleep each night, see only six clients per day, and spend at least one hour with my husband, talking and being together. I can't remember what the 5 stands for. What does that tell you about my mental health? Well, it tells me there is some boundary out there I'm not yet willing to see, absorb, and take seriously. In the meantime, I have plenty to keep working on with my 8, 6, and 1. I keep these numbers in mind as I make my daily boundary decisions.

"I like the four circles of Listening to Self and the applications, and it is something I want to work on."

"I can express my self to others."

"I just knew it was right [to leave] . . . back there doing my same old routine . . . like a nursemaid."

"I can really hear him talk. I realized I need to slow down and listen."

"Can my daughter say she is feeling more heard by me?"

"I kept my mouth shut. I didn't let it bury me."

"I did not want her to be there. She would offer me no comfort."

"I'm going to write my self a letter to remind my self. . ."

"I have my limits."

On **Developing Spirituality**

"Life has a way of ramping up, and moments of getting away and taking stock and redirecting are really lovely . . . They draw me into deeper work with myself and a more thoughtful way of living."

"The hopelessness of trying to fix myself without my higher power's help is an important concept to me."

As for **Spirituality**, I feel much more connected to my spiritual self than I did twenty years ago. A primary reason for this growth is that my earlier work in recovery awakened me to the presence and importance of a power greater than my self. In my day-today life, prior to recovery, the thought of letting go of things beyond my control had never occurred to me. I had not thought to include my higher power so consciously in my activities. I was too busy running my own life and the lives of others. This spiritual awakening has truly remained with me and grown.

The practice of mindfulness has continued to help me a great deal in this spiritual growth. My ability to quiet my mind and return, over and over, to the present moment is a wonderful gift, and one obtained through the regular practice of paying attention to the activities of my mind and returning my focus to the sensations within me and around me. This mindfulness enables me to feel more spacious and lets in many wonders, understandings, and experiences I could have never created for my self. When I am entangled, I am tight, closed, and hanging on. When I practice mindfulness, I am open, loose, quiet, and free. This freedom is the door that opens me to increased spirituality.

In the spirit of this calm openness, I am living more and more in the flow of life. I am not always there, but I sure know when I am. When I am in the flow of life, things go smoothly and easily. I'm not trying to make something happen. I'm not trying to make someone do something. Instead, through my quietly being and quietly seeing, the next thing happens or not, opens or not. I do my part and let go. I quietly be and quietly see some more, connecting with and trusting my spiritual self and my higher power whom I continue to get to know and welcome into my daily life. And on my life goes . . .

> *"The slowing down aspect of my weekend—stopping, breathing, listening, and writing—was invaluable to me. I particularly enjoyed the periods of silence and alone time."*

> *"Nothing I could do about nothing."*

"I can really only rely on my self and my higher power."

"God knows, and I have learned, that uncertainty is a Holy Place."

"I am making more time for just me."

"I love my self enough to get in the garden."

"I see my higher power as my ally."

Practices for Daily Living

"Entanglements are always there if we are not conscious," says a dear and wise client of mine. Yes, my experience is that I can get caught up in someone or something fairly easily, despite my work with my self on this. Only by being in the present with my feelings, thoughts, and experiences can I catch my self when I'm about to fall or perhaps already have. This is the consciousness of which my client speaks. With this consciousness, I then work with my self to regain and retain my center, employing these daily practices.

Living in the Now

"I can still remember every detail of the strawberry I mindfully ate. I am striving to continue mindfulness and check in with myself often."

I notice how many times I use the word "now." It's become a central concept for me in my life and work. I have come a long way in learning to live in the now; it has taken conscious practice. I had always been about planning ahead, looking forward to or worrying about things in the future. I could fret about, keep going

237

over, or wish I had done something different about things past. I can still fall into these ways in a heartbeat. It is my awareness of these behaviors of mine, and my intentional reconnecting with my breath, my spirit, and all that is within me and around me at the moment, that help me to live in the now—which is where I want to be.

Living in the now greatly facilitates disentangling. For the most part, I am not entangled if I come back to the now. A number of my entanglements involve projections into the future about what someone else's words or behaviors may ultimately mean or cause. Other entanglements involve my mixing what has happened to me in the past with what is happening now. Either way, adding the future or the past to the present is likely to entangle me.

Living in the now also helps me to disentangle if, despite my best efforts, I still feel entangled. When I bring my self to the now, I can hear what the other person is saying without adding my own twists. If I do add my own twists, I can be aware of them, feel them, acknowledge them, and check them out with the other person, always coming back to now—over and over.

Well-Defined by Me

"What is it that you are working on for your self?"

"For the first time I was connected with what was going on within me, and that was okay."

That's it! That's one of the greatest gifts that has come to me through this journey of mine: I am glad and grateful to be me. I know me much better. I listen to me. I return to me over and over. I wander out into the old, familiar world of watching and waiting for others, of wondering what they're thinking, what they want, trying to tell them what is best for them, trying to fix what's not mine to fix—see how easily I reel off this list! And then I catch my self doing any number of these things and I return to me, a place even more soothing than being with close friends. I listen to what I feel and want, and oblige when possible. I feel calmer, happier, and connected to the present.

In the past I was not well-defined, I was well-defended. I was holding on for dear life to ideas of how I was and should be. Let anyone offer me criticism or friendly feedback, and I'd feel threatened and defensive. I would not necessarily show these feelings in dramatic ways, but they were there. And later, as the day wore on, these feelings would turn into self-doubt and worry. My defensiveness made it close to impossible for me to use the feedback in any constructive way and eroded my struggling self further.

In the past I was defined by things outside my self: external events and attributes, the history of things I had done, what other people said and did to me, and how they reacted to me. My happiness and sense of self were based far more on relationships than I wanted to believe. They were based especially on the condition, or my perception of the condition, of my intimate relationships.

I am different than that now, when I am in good form.

I am now, at least, better defined by me.

We can come to know our self if we do not give most of our self away to someone else or to some activity in our life, defining our self primarily through our success or failure with that relationship or activity. To illustrate what I mean by being well-defined by me—connecting within, trusting who I am and what is important to me, letting that self-knowledge be the basis of my healthy self—I'll present a list I wrote in my journal almost twenty years ago while working on my recovery program. I am grateful for the items on this list and for the ways they continue to help me know and care for my self:

> *I am happy that I have such a lovely daughter, who I love and who loves me, and whose company I enjoy so much and who enjoys my company.*
>
> *I am happy with my old clapboard home that faces on a creek and river and not on a road.*
>
> *I love the wildness of my yard and the amateur gardening I do around here.*
>
> *I love being together as a family.*
>
> *I am happy that my parents have both lived as long as they have, and that they are healthy enough to live in their own home, have us visit, and share our lives.*
>
> *I appreciate the ways my brother cares for my parents and for me.*
>
> *I am happy with my work, my work colleagues, and the freedom I have to schedule my self as I do and to take long trips with my family.*
>
> *I am happy that I can travel and see places and people, happy that I was raised as a camper and so know how to travel on low budgets and do wonderful things.*
>
> *I love that I have my health, and that I have been able to be an amateur dancer all these years. I am at a great studio with a teacher and classes I love.*

I have been extremely blessed with strong Al-Anon meetings near me, and I feel so at home with many of the members. It is truly a place I can comfortably be me.

I love my circle of friends here in the county. It is nice to spend these years together raising our children, growing in our own lives, and just plain having fun.

I love my animals and value their companionship in my life.

I am happy that I am able to be by my self and have such a good time.

I am more confident about my self and my work, and am feeling increasingly creative.

Now, having spent nearly twenty more years with my self, deepening my work, I add:

I appreciate the person I am —

> *with my strengths and weaknesses,*
>
> *with my intelligence and humor,*
>
> *with my kindness and impatience,*
>
> *with my curiosity and creativity.*

I am a work-in-progress — a handful, as I am known to say — as I live with me and keep growing.

Quietly Be. Quietly See. Anchored in Me.

"I reach out by first reaching within and knowing what I have to offer."

Nancy at age sixty-seven

Let us now return to "Quietly Be. Quietly See." As I said in that passage at the end of Chapter Two, I value this suggestion that I quietly be and quietly see what is going on with me and my relationship with someone else before I jump in and try to manage, control, or fix something, or before I try to express to them my feelings and needs, which may not be usefully clear to me in the moment of entanglement. In that moment, I may not yet be ready to accept that I may or may not get what I am asking for. So I hold steady with my self in the present in a supportive, listening way.

Twenty-or-so years later, I am adding Anchored in Me to that passage.

I now see that, on the occasion of that story, I did not clarify to my husband that I wanted more contact with him. He probably thought we were simply watching television. He did not know I thought we might be doing something else, like having a conversation, and I was not able to express my self to him in the moment. My insecure self was present. She did not want to create an argument or upset the evening by speaking up. My insecure self was not able or willing to be more direct with him. So rather than express myself, I took my bothered, insecure self to bed.

I was not yet able to anchor in my self.

Quietly being was probably the best thing for me to do at that point, considering my level of recovery. Quietly being is neither a pout nor a retreat, but rather a quiet presence that fosters the detachment needed to respond, not react. It calms and centers, and we see our self and our situation more fully and accurately. It allows us to connect with our spirit, which I believe is there all the time just waiting for our return.

Through this quietly being and quietly seeing, I am able to connect with my mind, feelings, body, and spirit. I am able to clarify what it is that is bothering me, and what I want or need. I am able to find my "I" statements, and determine boundaries I may need to state. I let go to my higher power, remembering that I am not in full control, and may not know what is best in a particular situation. All of this helps me to develop my healthy self, to know who I am, to care for her, and to be able to speak for her. I want to have this relationship with my self and then be able to stay anchored in me as I interact with the other person.

Anchored in Me. It is so essential to our growth that it merits inclusion in this suggested way of living: Quietly Be. Quietly See. Anchored in Me.

"Anchored in me" means having a clear understanding and commitment to my self—mind, feelings, body, and spirit—and staying connected with these as I express my self to someone else. An anchor holds the boat in place. The boat may be rocking some, moving around a bit, depending on the length of rope attached. The boat stays within the range of its anchoring, sometimes pulled to the far edges perhaps, but not beyond. If we happen to be on that boat, we trust the anchor to keep us safe and where we want to be.

This anchoring of my self is not rigid. Like the boat, I have some range in which I am anchored, allowing my self to hear the other person, consider what they are saying, and remember the relationship I have (or want to have) with them. But as I do this listening, I do not pull up my anchor and float away with them, leaving the healthy connection with my self behind as we drift into the fog.

My secure self has grown over these years of recovery. By secure I mean being able to listen to my self, attune to my feelings and needs, and know that I will be there for me. I am better at expressing what I want and what I feel, and accepting whatever response I may get. I anchor in me. I remember why I said what I said, quiet my judgments and fears, and check in with my self once again before I continue the conversation. Rather than losing my self in the conversation and the relationship, I am strengthening my self and my ability to be true to me.

Such growth is available to each of us. A sustained and loving connection with our secure, healthy self helps us to not become lost in someone else as we have in the past. We may feel lost at times, but with steady, reliable work we can develop the skills to find our way out of our lostness, cultivating more profoundly a self that we know, love, trust, honor, protect, encourage, and can rely on for direction and strength, for greater health and happiness, and for the blessing of serenity. It is that self—*your* self—that is with you now, ready and able to help you keep finding your way.

Family Roles as Described by Claudia Black in *It Will Never Happen to Me* (2002)

THE RESPONSIBLE CHILD

Strengths	Deficits
• Organized	• Inability to listen
• Leadership skills	• Inability to follow
• Decision-maker	• Inability to play
• Initiator	• Inability to relax
• Perfectionist	• Inflexibility
• Goal-oriented	• Need to be right
• Self-discipline	• Severe need to be in control
	• Extreme fear of mistakes
	• Lack of spontaneity

THE ADJUSTER

Strengths	Deficits
• Flexibility	• Inability to initiate
• Ability to follow	• Fear of making decisions
• Easygoing attitude	• Lack of direction
• Not upset by negative situations	• Inability to perceive options, power
	• Follow without questioning

THE PLACATER

Strengths	Deficits
• Caring	• Inability to receive
• Empathetic	• Inability to focus on self
• Good listener	• Guilty
• Sensitive to others	• Strong fear of anger
• Gives well	• High tolerance for inappropriate behavior
• Nice smile	
• Warm	

THE ACTING-OUT CHILD

Strengths	Deficits
• Close to own feelings	• Inability to initiate
• Less denial, greater honesty	• Fear of making decisions
• Creative	• Lack of direction
• Sense of humor	• Inability to perceive options, power
• Ability to lead without questioning	• Follow without questioning (truancy, addiction, high school dropout, teen pregnancy, etc.)

Roles in an Alcoholic Family (Wegscheider-Cruse, 1989)

System Dynamics of the Alcoholic Family

MOTIVATING FEELING	IDENTIFYING SYMPTOMS	PAYOFF		POSSIBLE PRICE
		For individual	For family	
DEPENDENT				
Shame	Chemical use	Relief of pain	None	Addiction
ENABLER				
Anger	Powerlessness	Importance; self-righteousness	Responsibility	Illness; "martyrdom"
HERO				
Inadequacy; guilt	Overachievement	Attention (positive)	Self-worth	Compulsive drive
SCAPEGOAT				
Hurt	Delinquency	Attention (negative)	Focus away from dependent	Self-destruction; addiction
LOST CHILD				
Loneliness	Solitariness; shyness	Escape	Relief	Social isolation
MASCOT				
Fear	Clowning; hyperactivity	Attention (amused)	Fun	Immaturity; emotional illness

Reprinted by permission of the author(s) and publisher: *Another Chance*, Second Ed., Sharon Wegscheider-Cruse, Science & Behavior Books, Inc.

Characteristics of an Adult Child of an Alcoholic (Woitiz, 1990)

1. Adult children of alcoholics guess at what normal behavior is.

2. Adult children of alcoholics have difficulty following a project through from beginning to end.

3. Adult children of alcoholics lie when it would be just as easy to tell the truth.

4. Adult children of alcoholics judge themselves without mercy.

5. Adult children of alcoholics have difficulty having fun.

6. Adult children of alcoholics take themselves very seriously.

7. Adult children of alcoholics have difficulty with intimate relationships.

8. Adult children of alcoholics overreact to changes over which they have no control.

9. Adult children of alcoholics constantly seek approval and affirmation.

10. Adult children of alcoholics usually feel that they are different from other people.

11. Adult children of alcoholics are super responsible or super irresponsible.

12. Adult children of alcoholics are extremely loyal, even in the face of evidence that the loyalty is undeserved.

13. Adult children of alcoholics are impulsive. They tend to lock themselves into a course of action without giving serious consideration to alternative behaviors or possible consequences. This impulsivity leads to confusion, self-loathing, and loss of control over their environment. In addition, they spend an excessive amount of energy cleaning up the mess.

Illustration of Neurobiology and Self (Johnston, 2015)

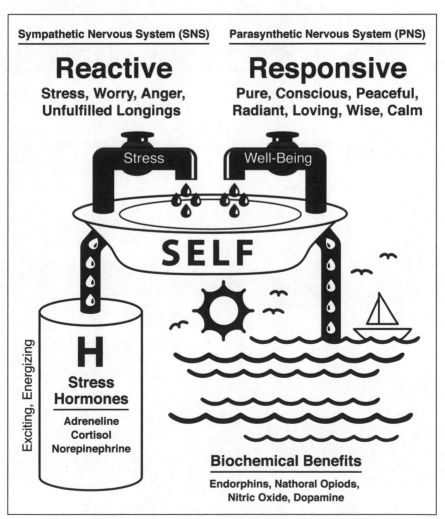

Illustrated by Nancy L. Johnston, MS, LPC, LSATP – nancyljohnston.com
From the Writings of Rick Hanson, author of Buddha's Brain & Hardwiring Happiness.

Chart for Healthy Emotional Expression (Johnston, 2014)

Pathways to Emotional Health

FEELING	AWARENESS	CHOICES

Chaperone/Be With
- Thich Nhat Hanh
- Mindful presence

Cues/Signals
- Self-Care
- HALT

Feeling

Become Aware

Recognize

Contain

Communicate
- To safe others
- To person it involves: Assertiveness

Identify

Change Neutral Structure
- Negativity bias to positivity
- Let the good seep in

Nancy L. Johnston, MS, LPC, LSATP – Codependence Camp, Spring 2013; Spring 2014; Fall 2015

Continuum of Expressive Behaviors (Johnston, 1995)

Continuum of Behaviors

PASSIVE	ASSERTIVE	AGGRESSIVE
withdraws avoids hides silent goes along	"I" statements clearly expressing your feelings, needs, thoughts. Elaborate justifications and explanations are not needed. "Broken record": Repetitions of your "I" statements may be the best way to respond to invitations and/or attacks to move your from your stated position.	forceful, pushy selfish hits yells threatens pushes breaks things curses name calls "You" statements accuses falsely accuses
Your emotions are ignored or not acknowledged.	You remain aware of your emotions and they are under your control.	Your emotions are out of your awareness and your control.
Your behavior shows no respect for yourself of the other.	Your behavior shows respect for yourself and the other.	Your behavior shows no respect for yourself or the other.

Compiled by Nancy L. Johnston, Licensed Professional Counselor, Staunton and Lexington, Virginia

Ainsworth, Mary D. S., and Silvia M. Bell. "Attachment, Exploration, and Separation: Illustrated by the Behavior of One-Year-Olds in a Strange Situation." *Child Development 41*, no. 1 (1970): 49–67.

Ainsworth, Mary D. S., Mary C. Blehar, Everett Waters, and Sally N. Wall. *Patterns of Attachment: A Psychological Study of the Strange Situation.* New York: Psychology Press, 2015.

Al-Anon Family Group Headquarters, Inc. *Detachment* (brochure). Virginia Beach, VA: Al-Anon Family Group Headquarters, 1981.

———. *One Day at a Time in Al-Anon.* Virginia Beach, VA: Al-Anon Family Group Headquarters, 1987.

———. *Courage to Change: One Day at a Time in Al-Anon II.* Virginia Beach, VA: Al-Anon Family Group Headquarters, 1992.

Alcoholics Anonymous World Services, Inc. *Alcoholics Anonymous*, 4th ed. New York: AA World Services, 2002.

American Psychological Association. "The Road to Resilience." American Psychological Association. https://www.apa.org/helpcenter/road-resilience

American Psychiatric Association. *Diagnostic and Statistical Manual of Mental Disorders*, 5th ed. Washington, DC: American Psychiatric Association, 2013.

Bartholomew, Kim, and Leonard M. Horowitz. "Attachment Styles among Young Adults: A Test of a Four-Category Model." *Journal of Personality and Social Psychology* 61, no. 2 (1991): 226–44.

Beattie, Melody. *Codependent No More: How to Stop Controlling Others and Start Caring for Yourself.* Center City, MN: Hazelden, 1987.

———. *The Language of Letting Go: Daily Meditations for Codependents.* San Francisco: Harper & Row, 1990.

———. *The New Codependency: Help and Guidance for Today's Generation.* New York: Simon & Schuster, 2009.

Black, Claudia. *It Will Never Happen to Me: Growing Up with Addiction as Youngsters, Adolescents, Adults.* Center City, MN: Hazelden, 2002.

Bowlby, John. *A Secure Base: Clinical Applications of Attachment Theory.* London: Routledge, 1988.

Bowen, Murray. *Family Therapy in Clinical Practice.* New York: J. Aronson, 1978.

Bray, James H., Donald S. Williamson, and Paul E. Malone. "Personal Authority in the Family System: Development of a Questionnaire to Measure Personal Authority in Intergenerational Family Processes." *Journal of Marital and Family Therapy* 10, no. 2 (1984): 167–78.

Brooks, Jeanne. *Crisis Intervention: The Neurobiology of Crisis.* CreateSpace Independent Publishing Platform, 2017.

Central Recovery Press. *Discover Recovery.* Las Vegas, NV: Central Recovery Press, 2017.

Cermak, Timmen L. *Diagnosing and Treating Co-Dependence: A Guide for Professionals who Work with Chemical Dependents, Their Spouses, and Children.* Minneapolis: Johnson Institute Books, 1986.

Co-Dependents Anonymous International. "Patterns and Characteristics of Codependence." CoDA, 2011. http://coda.org/index.cfm/meeting-materials1/patterns-and-characteristics-2011/_

Courtois, Christine A., and Julian D. Ford, eds. *Treating Complex Traumatic Stress Disorders: An Evidence-Based Guide.* New York: Guilford Press, 2009.

Dear, Greg E., Clare M. Roberts, and Lois Lange. "Defining Codependency: A Thematic Analysis of Published Definitions." In *Advances in Psychology Research,* vol. 34, edited by Serge P. Shohov, 189–205. Huntington, NY: Nova Science Publishers, 2005.

Dear, Greg E., and Clare M. Roberts. "Validation of the Holyoake Codependency Index." *The Journal of Psychology* 139, no. 4 (2005): 293–313.

Drews, Toby R. *Getting Them Sober*, vol. 1. South Plainfield, NJ: Bridge Publishing, 1980.

———. *Getting Them Sober,* vol. 4. Baltimore: Recovery Communications, 1992.

Felitti, Vincent J., Robert F. Anda, Dale Nordenberg, David F. Williamson, Alison M. Spitz, Valerie Edwards, Mary P. Koss, and James S. Marks. "Relationship of Childhood Abuse and Household Dysfunction to Many of the Leading Causes of Death in Adults: The Adverse Childhood Experiences (ACE) Study." *American Journal of Preventive Medicine* 14, no. 4 (1998): 245–58.

Hanson, Rick. *Buddha's Brain: The Practical Neuroscience of Happiness, Love, and Wisdom.* Oakland, CA: New Harbinger, 2009.

———. *Hardwiring Happiness: The New Brain Science of Contentment, Calm, and Confidence.* New York: Harmony, 2013.

Hazan, Cindy, and Phillip Shaver. "Romantic Love Conceptualized as an Attachment Process." *Journal of Personality and Social Psychology* 52, no. 3 (1987): 511–24.

Holzel, Britta K., James Carmody, Mark Vangel, Christina Congleton, Sita M. Yerramsetti, Tim Gard, and Sara W. Lazar. "Mindfulness Practice Leads to Increases in Regional Brain Gray Matter Density." *Psychiatry Research* 191, no. 1 (2011): 36–43.

Johnston, Nancy L. *My Life as a Border Collie: Freedom from Codependency.* Las Vegas, NV: Central Recovery Press, 2011.

Kabat-Zinn, Jon. *Wherever You Go, There You Are*, 10th ed. New York: Hachette, 2005.

———. *Full Catastrophe Living*, rev. ed. New York: Bantam, 2013.

Kübler-Ross, Elisabeth. *On Death and Dying.* New York: Macmillan, 1969.

McKay, Matthew, Jeffrey C. Wood, and Jeffrey Brantley. *The Dialectical Behavior Therapy Skills Workbook*. Oakland, CA: New Harbinger, 2007.

Main, Mary, and Judith Solomon. "Discovery of an Insecure-Disorganized/Disoriented Attachment Pattern." In *Affective Development in Infancy*, edited by T. Berry Brazelton and Michael W. Yogman, 95–124. Norwood, NJ: Ablex, 1986.

Maslow, A. H. "A Theory of Human Motivation." *Psychological Review* 50, no. 4 (1943): 370–96.

Miller, Alice. *The Drama of the Gifted Child: The Search for the True Self*. New York: Basic Books, 1981.

Nhat Hanh, Thich. *Peace Is Every Step: The Path of Mindfulness in Everyday Life*. New York: Bantam, 1991.

———. *The Miracle of Mindfulness: A Manual on Meditation*. Boston: Beacon Press, 1999.

Norwood, Robin. *Women Who Love Too Much: When You Keep Wishing and Hoping He'll Change*, reprint ed. New York: Pocket Books, 2008.

Prest, Layne A., and Howard Protinsky. "Family Systems Theory: A Unifying Framework for Codependence." *The American Journal of Family Therapy* 21, no. 4 (1993): 352–60.

Prochaska, James O., and Carlo C. DiClemente. "Stages and Processes of Self-Change of Smoking: Toward an Integrative Model of Change. *Journal of Consulting and Clinical Psychology* 51, no. 3 (1983): 390–95.

Rotter, Julian B. *Social Learning and Clinical Psychology*. New York: Prentice-Hall, 1954.

Wegscheider-Cruse, Sharon. *Another Chance: Hope and Health for the Alcoholic Family*, 2nd ed. Palo Alto, CA: Science & Behavior Books, 1989.

Woititz, Janet G. *Adult Children of Alcoholics*, expanded ed. Pompano Beach, FL: Health Communications, 1990.